MISSING PIECES

MISSING PIECES

Derek Sorrell

Mynd Matters Publishing
715 Peachtree Street NE
Suites 100 & 200
Atlanta, GA 30308

e-ISBN: 978-1-953307-74-3
ISBN: 978-1-953307-73-6 (pbk)
ISBN: 978-1-953307-72-9 (hdcv)

To my late mother, Eloise Sorrell,
whose impact on my life can never be filled.
I'll never be the same.

Introduction

A parent, for the most part, is supposed to take care of their child(ren) to the best of their abilities given their resources and knowledge. Parents with little money or poor job opportunities are limited in what they can provide to a child although most, if not all, parents want their children to be in better situations and have more opportunities than they had growing up. For some parents, it is about creating opportunities that will decrease the chances for the child to struggle as an adult.

For me, the problem came when I realized my child was atypical. I will attempt to explain how my ignorance for my child's needs hindered his growth and progression, as well as my own. At the time, I believed I was doing and being a good parent. I thought because I loved my son, all of my wrongdoings as a parent were excusable. But they weren't and the worst problem—no one around me knew anything about parenting either.

My parents, even in my adulthood and parenthood, are the biggest reasons I made it through the troubled years.

I know plenty of people who complain about their struggles with their "normal" children. Before reaching this point in my life, I was often envious of those people and would have traded lives in an instant.

In this writing, I will attempt to discuss many sensitive topics I have dealt with while caring for my son. Mainly, the intersection of abuse, guilt, and mental illness. I hope to also be a reference for aspiring and current parents. Definitely a tale of what not to do! Be advised, I am not an expert on autism but am a parent of a beautiful child with autism. For years, I failed to fully understand my son and his needs. It took over a decade to seek help as a parent. But even with more clarity, it is not enough. We must continue to search for more help and answers.

1.

I should probably give a bit of back story about Tanya (my son, Tarek's, mom). In 2004, Tanya and I met in Valdosta, Georgia. I was twenty-years old and Tanya was nine years my senior. We were part of the team setting up the inside of the new location for a national retail chain. Although Tanya, a certified optician, had worked for the company in the Eye Center for about nine years, we'd never met. You could describe me as a chubby scrub. I barely kept a job and happened to meet her because the retailer was having a job fair and I fell into the role.

I remember the first time I saw her. Every day, everyone in the store would come to the front and gather while the managers gave their talk. I rarely paid attention to anything said in those meetings. They were more a way for me and the guys to check out our women coworkers. We'd spend the time trying to figure out who we were going to try to get numbers from, etc.

Tanya had a pair of lime green or yellow green joggers with a white strip down the side. She had a matching tank top shirt and a white head wrap tied in a bun. She stood out because she was pretty and curvaceous. I would wait until she walked away before I would leave, so I could watch her walk away. I never got the courage to speak to her until after the store opened.

At work, I always hung out with my boys, Haywood and David. They were older and we used to sit in the break room and talk to the girls coming in and out. I was never a big ladies' man, like most of the other guys. I remember hanging out with David and Haywood playing basketball at the park then we would go to David's house to drink and chill. I can't remember if David was married or not, but he was definitely in a relationship. Occasionally, he and his girlfriend would have friends over. One of the girls that would stop by worked at the store with us. I think she liked me but I'm not sure. But that was my luck with women. Someone was either using me, or I would be a second or third choice to friends of mine.

Initially, I had to watch Tanya attempt to shoot her shot with David. If I remember correctly, Tanya may have even asked me to hook her up with David. Being the good homeboy that I am, I relayed the message to him. He smirked about it but never showed her much interest. I felt like I wasn't going to ever get with her, so I constantly hyped up David to get with her. In a way, I was trying to live vicariously through him. I once said, "Man, you gonna get Tanya man! She thick!" David was like, "Nah, you holler at her."

I probably pondered the thought of shooting my shot with her for about a week. Until one day, we were all on break together in the break room. Tanya was sitting and talking to another female colleague. I don't remember what they were discussing, I was just waiting for my moment to shoot my shot. I may have even blurted it out, "Aye Tanya, when you gonna let me call you?" She asked my age after that. I was like *damn, should I lie?* But I told the truth. Like most people, she didn't believe I was my age. I've always been a big guy, so most people assumed I was older. But to my disbelief, Tanya still gave me her number.

Being young and dumb, you to tend to be shown signs of things, good or bad, and you choose to ignore them based on being blinded by something. My blindness came from sex and attention. After roughly one week of dating, Tanya's ex-boyfriend decided he wanted her back. At the time, I was living in Lakeland, Georgia which is roughly eighteen miles from Valdosta. Apparently, Tanya's ex was upset that she was dating someone else. In attempt to see her, he banged on her door screaming and yelling. He was hitting the door so hard, he dented it.

So, me, being a young bull, not interested in losing the most sex and female attention I was getting at the time, drove to Valdosta to save the day in case he decided to come back. After making sure she was okay, she told me he wanted to confront me. Well of course I couldn't punk out. When he came back, I initiated the confrontation with him. Luckily for the both of us, it was just verbal. Little did he know, I had a knife in my pocket with the blade already unfolded. I actually contemplated stabbing him before he even tried to swing because I was so nervous.

I think my size caught him off guard. Back then, I was

about 6'2 285lbs. So we stood outside and talked about how he felt. It was a weird conversation. Me, a twenty-one-year-old, having to tell someone well into their thirties that they're acting juvenile. I explained to him that if she does not want to be with him anymore, he can't change it and needs to move on. He actually agreed with me. He continued to explain that he and Tanya had a lot of history. He warned me to be careful with her. I assumed he was trying to slander her character so he could have her back. He told me she was extremely lazy, doesn't clean, and is not self-motivated to do anything. He said everything she had came from him. I listened but what I was getting from her and how I felt back then far outweighed what he was saying.

Shortly after that incident, I moved in with Tanya and enjoyed every minute of it because we never argued, she seemed to do whatever I asked or wanted, and we had sex often. I was more than happy.

Bedroom conversations led to Tanya explaining that she'd been pregnant when she was sixteen years old and had an abortion. In the process of the abortion, her tubes became clogged or something which prevented her from getting pregnant with her ex.

Six to eight months into our relationship, I hadn't made any definitive plans to have a baby, however I wasn't opposed to the thought. I was happy as I could be. Tanya went to the doctor for a procedure to check things out with her tubes. For the procedure, the doctor injected a dye into the fallopian tubes in order to see if there was any blockage, which there was.

Time went by. I took Tanya to meet my family and I talked to her family on the phone. She was originally from the St. Louis area.

Her menstrual cycles were always irregular. I honestly never used protection when we had sex, especially after she explained that she could not get pregnant.

One day, Tanya told me she was extremely late for her monthly cycle. Me being a man, I didn't think much of it. I don't think I even responded. There were times before when she was late and she took a pregnancy test just to make sure she wasn't pregnant. This time, she got out of the shower and took a test. After waiting for the results, she went into the bathroom and checked the tester. I noticed her acting a little weird when she came out. She acted as if she did not look at the test. So I walked into the bathroom and saw that it showed positive. I immediately ran out of the bathroom and asked/told her she was pregnant. Seeming shocked, Tanya also expressed happiness in the moment.

Tanya and I had not been together a full year and were expecting our first child. My immaturity and insecurities kept me from processing how long other people may have dated prior to marriage and having kids. But I knew I did not want to feel left out.

I was mature for my age in a lot of ways, based on my want to take care of Tanya and ensuring she didn't want for anything. I provided for her as much as I could with what I had. You couldn't tell me I was not being a man, even though I swapped jobs like I changed underwear. I cooked most of our meals and did a majority of the cleaning as well.

Even though now when I look back, I realize I didn't do enough of that.

We lived in a one-bedroom apartment with a lot of clutter. We would put aside dishes that needed to be cleaned and allow clothes to pile up. We lived in a mess, honestly. I still lived as the immature boy that I was. I felt like I was finally free to do as I pleased with the person I was with since I paid bills at my own place. I was far from the man I thought I was.

With Tanya pregnant and us living together, I married her in under a year. As the pregnancy furthered, we eventually moved across town to a townhome. By that time, I was working for a bottling company as a delivery driver. Tanya and I later found out we were having a boy. We made list after list of potential names for our son eventually coming up with the name Tarek, a blend of our two names—TA-nya and De-REK.

As Tanya began showing, she enjoyed more and more the physical feelings and emotions that came with bearing a child. She often over-ate thinking she would need to feed the baby often, only to eventually lose weight later in the pregnancy from becoming more fatigued. I used to make 1AM runs to Krystal's for her to take one bite from a sandwich or I would go to Walmart for a weird flavor of Ben and Jerry's ice cream and she would eat half a spoonful.

My mother and father were excited and expecting their first grandchild and wanted nothing but the best for him. They bought clothes and most of the vital things we needed to get by as parents. My mom and dad didn't want me to struggle or face the same complications they had growing up. Even though their grandson was not born yet, they were already a big part of his life.

In our new home, both bedrooms were upstairs. When Tanya did not feel able to make it up the stairs, we would occasionally sleep downstairs. She on the sofa and me on the floor. At that time, I didn't require Tanya to do much around the house because I did not want to put stress on her if I didn't have to. I worked Monday through Friday with long hours but was making good money.

My mother was the first Black assistant principle and worked her way up to be the first Black superintendent in Lanier County. My father was the first Black men's basketball head coach in Lanier County. He is like a local legend from his high school days and his current coaching days. Both had been teaching for thirty years.

Oddly enough, the night that changed everything was a home basketball game. Tanya and I were in attendance on the home side with my mother. Tanya was about six and half months pregnant. While we watched the game, she repeatedly said that Tarek was moving like crazy. I assumed it was the noise that was making Tarek go crazy inside Tanya's stomach.

The next morning, Tanya and I woke up in our bedroom. I began moving around in the bed, when I noticed the bed was wet and Tanya's underwear was wet as well. I asked her if she pee'd in the bed. Of course, she denied it, so I jokingly ridiculed her about it.

Tanya got up and changed her clothes. After being up,

she was in and out of the bathroom. She explained that she felt like she was urinating, but she did not have the usual sensation that comes with it. I took Tanya to the local hospital to see if there was a problem. After testing the fluid that Tanya was excreting, the test showed that the fluid was amniotic fluid. Tanya's amniotic sac had ruptured.

After that incident, Tanya was placed on bedrest. If I remember correctly, Tanya was then sent to a hospital in Macon, Georgia. I went with her initially, only to return home to work and provide for our family. I don't remember exactly how long she was there, but I remember being at work when I received the call that changed my life forever. I was informed that the doctor was inducing Tanya because it would be too risky not to induce. Macon is 152 miles from Valdosta. After dropping my truck off at work and hitting the road, it took me maybe an hour and fifteen minutes to drive to her. I was going ninety miles an hour most of the way.

I pulled into the parking deck and ran to the labor and delivery area. Running down the hallway, I saw a sign for the NICU. I didn't know at the time, but soon, I would become extremely familiar with that specific room.

I might have been in the hallway for about fifteen or twenty minutes. I inadvertently stood in front of a big wooden door. A few nurses ran inside and then Tanya's doctor walked into the same room while talking to another doctor. Then it sank in who may be inside the room where all the commotion was happening. The door opened again, and I could see two nurses standing over a station appearing to be doing CPR. I knew then that my child was in trouble.

I continued to wait patiently in the hallway until someone came and told me what was going on or Tarek came rolling out to me. I didn't really care what happened as long as he was alive.

$2.$

The door opened, and the nurse pushed out a cart with an incubator on it. As she walked by, I glanced inside seeing Tarek lying there with tubes in his mouth. He had an awkward alignment to his jaw. To this day, I can still picture that moment so clearly.

The nurse stopped and asked if I was the father. Even though I had a feeling the child in the incubator was my son, she confirmed it for me and told me for ten minutes, he didn't take a breath. Then, finally, he'd started breathing. I was happy that my son was finally here. My little mini me. Tarek was born two months early, but nothing could ruin that moment.

I saw Tanya after the delivery. I kissed her on the forehead and as she woke up, she exhaled into my face. My eyes watered up and we stood by until a nurse came in to explain what all had happened.

Apparently, while in the womb, Tarek's umbilical cord got wrapped around his neck and he began to choke. In delivery, Tarek was coming out butt first and the doctor had to reposition his body. While trying to reposition his body, the doctor made the call to perform an emergency C-section.

They explained that Tarek came out unconscious and the nursing staff performed CPR for ten minutes before they were able to get Tarek breathing. The doctor explained that Tarek would have to have testing done, due to possible complications that may stem from blood not reaching the brain while he wasn't breathing. We knew it would be a long road ahead of us but I felt I was ready for whatever was to come.

When I got the call to come down to the NICU, I was ecstatic. I got to see my little man and hopefully hold him. I didn't run down but I walked briskly as hell. Once I got to the door, I rang the doorbell. I hated how some nurses get so used to their job, they forget everyone doesn't know the process. I'm standing at the speaker excited, only to hear,

"May I help you?"

"Yes ma'am, I'm here to see my son."

"Name?"

"Derek Sorrell!"

"Baby's name?"

"Tarek Sorrell."

"Come in and wash your hands at the sink before continuing to the floor please."

Hell, just the interrogation at the speaker had me deflated by the time I stepped inside the doors.

As I entered the NICU, the first thing I heard was several babies crying at once. I stood in the doorway surveying the room. Nurses walking back and forth from station to station. One of the nurses from the nurses' station yelled to me, "Please wash your hands before entering! Soap is on the sink!"

Damn these nurses don't have any manners, I thought. I continued to the sink and got some of the soap. I remember the soap because when I began to rub it in, I could feel the alcohol in it.

Tarek's station was in the middle of the room, maybe the second or third station from the nurses' station. As the nurses tended to him, I heard him cry for the first time. I didn't realize it earlier but Tarek was tiny. He was a fighter though. His diapers were the size of sliced cheese. The nurse changed his little diaper and attempted to turn him over on his stomach and he actually stretched his arms out preventing her from putting him on his stomach. I'm pretty sure she could have done it if she wanted to, but it showed how strong he was.

She weighed him as two pounds and fifteen ounces. I forgot how long he was but compared to the size of my hands, Tarek was about the length of one and half of my hands. They had to put him under the UV light for a couple of days for a reason that I quickly forgot. I just know I could not hold him just yet.

Even though I couldn't hold him, it didn't deter me from seeing him. Tanya could not see him due to an infection she got from her C-section wound. I was in the NICU every day from the beginning of visitation to the end while Tanya slept all day. I didn't want to miss a moment.

While I was there, I actually befriended some of the other parents. I also grew attached to other kids from a distance. Before getting to Tarek's station, there was a baby in the incubator screaming to the top of his lungs every day.

He had a little colostomy bag attached. I don't know how old he was, but I know if you made eye contact with him, his eyes would stare through you as he appeared to be screaming in pain. As I stared at him, on one instance, a nurse explained that his mother was a frequent drug user and the child's intestines did not develop properly. I never saw that child's parent or parents the entire time Tarek was in the hospital.

Whenever I would visit Tarek I always saw one of the hospital social workers come into the unit. The nurses called him Charlie. Charlie was in a wheelchair. He might have been disabled in some way, but from what I could tell, he didn't lack in intelligence or character. He must have been charming or funny because the women loved talking to him. Later I found out that Charlie's job was to help needy families of children in the unit find resources. But unfortunately, I didn't find this out until later.

No words can ever explain my appreciation for the Ronald McDonald House. The Ronald House was about a block and a half down the road near the overpass. I was given information about House through one of the other parents in the NICU. I didn't have enough money to pay for a hotel and pay the bills at home. When I visited the Ronald McDonald House for the first time, the manager explained that they take donations for the duration of your stay at the home, however if you are not able to pay, you still were able to live there as long as you had a child in the NICU.

I loved that place, it was like a big bed and breakfast. Whenever you were hungry, you could go into the kitchen and make whatever you wanted with the items that were there. All the food was donated to the house. The families would often congregate in the kitchen and share stories about what led them there. To this day, if I ever donate any money to any organization, I donate to The Ronald McDonald home because of my first-hand experience with the organization.

Within the first couple of weeks, Tarek went through testing after testing to see if there was any damage due to the birth. When I received the results from the testing, I was at Tarek's station watching the nurse tend to him. The doctor came in and began giving me some hard news. I was told that Tarek had a grade four bleed on his brain. The doctor explained how serious the condition was. The most crushing new they shared was that Tarek probably would not make it through the month. I stopped listening to everything the doctor said after that. I think the only thing I heard was that they would continue to monitor the bleed to make sure it didn't worsen.

Even though the doctor, as a medical professional, had a job to do, I'm sure he could have explained the facts with more empathy. However, no parent wants to hear that they'll likely never get a chance to watch their child grow up so his words would've always been unwelcomed.

Most parents have dreams of the family they're creating when their child is born. Fathers dream of playing with their sons, teaching them to drive and be the men they know to be. But at that moment, a doctor was telling me that my dreams would probably never be a reality. He did mention a slim chance of Tarek making it through but all I saw were my dreams evaporating. I was furious by the news. *My first born will die.* Why wouldn't he just let me bask in my happiness of Tarek's presence?

I stared at Tarek through the clear plastic wall. He had on little eye covers and wires connected to his chest and feet. Tarek was also connected to a ventilator. His lungs were not developed enough to function on their own, so the machine had to breathe for him.

I cried for a couple of days. Whenever I looked at Tarek, I teared up. The first time I was able to touch him gave me life. For those who don't know how an incubator looks, imagine a plastic box with two arm holes on both sides. When the nurse asked if I wanted to touch my son, I looked at her with a nervous smile. He was smaller than a loaf of bread. I reached my hand through the arm hole and nudged his hand with my index finger. He appeared to be sleeping, but after nudging his hand, he lifted his hand and grabbed my finger. It was like a breath of life into me. It was also funny to see how small he was. Tarek's hands were so little. His fingertips touched the edge of my nail and the thumb wrapped halfway around the other side of my finger tip.

I was the only person visiting and spending time with Tarek because Tanya was pretty much quarantined from him. Outside of the womb, I was the first family member to see, touch, feed, hold, swaddle, and change Tarek.

The first time I held him made me more nervous than touching him, of course. The nurse made me sit in a rocking chair beside the bed as she draped a baby blanket over my shoulder. She swaddled Tarek in a blanket like a burrito and slowly placed him in my arms. This was by far the greatest moment in my life. I've held babies before, but when you hold your child, that you helped create, it's something special. I held him close to my heart to keep him warm and for him to listen to the beat of my chest hoping it soothed him so he didn't cry. The only thing that saddened the moment were the cords and wires attached to him.

Feeding Tarek was a task. His bottles were the size of small salt and pepper shakers. The nurse showed me how to assist him into pulling the nipple. I sat Tarek up on my lap. He was wrapped so tight, all I had to do was hold my hand at the back of his head to brace him. When I put the nipple of the bottle into his mouth, the nurse showed me a trick to help him eat. Most times, when I put the nipple in his mouth, Tarek would just hold it in place. Because the bottle was so small, you could use one of your other fingers to lift his chin up and down. This helped him learned how to drink his formula.

Since I was learning all the tricks and things to do with Tarek, I would eventually show Tanya and any other family visitors how and what to do. To me, I was creating a bond with my son that most men probably didn't initially.

As Tanya began to heal, she was still extremely sore from the wound. I had to assist her to and from the bathroom while she was in the hospital. I even helped wipe her butt too. I couldn't complain since I'd help put her in the situation. The nurse also showed me how to flush out her scar. Tanya had staples across her scar, but at the edge of it, you could open the wound and the nurse took a pointed bottle filled with saline solution and squirted to flush the wound.

I never thought of how things possibly could have affected Tanya while she was in the hospital. The pain medication probably kept her sedated to the point where she may not have had the opportunity to think about it. I was always in the NICU and when I'd come back to her room, I would tell her stories of things she could not see or do for herself. After Tanya was released from the hospital, she joined me at the Ronald McDonald House. I traveled back to Valdosta to work during the week and returned to my family on weekends.

As time went on, things got better with Tarek. After more testing, the bleed on his brain slowly diminished. Family began visiting the hospital. Everyone took turns enjoying the new member of our family. Tanya began visiting Tarek and learning how to handling a premature baby.

Tarek had been on the breathing machine for over a month or so. Little did we know, the bill was adding up. Honestly, I had no clue about hospital bills or anything. I didn't know what we would need when we got home or while we were there. I thought what we experienced was somewhat typical and the worse thing we had to deal with was the birth itself. Remember, I was only twenty-one or twenty-two at the time. I thought I was a man, but looking back, I didn't have a clue.

As Tarek progressed, the doctor explained to us that he

may have some delays as he got older. He further explained that Tarek could have some disabilities but I didn't give a damn. As long as we took him home and treated him like a "normal" child, he will be as normal as we treated him. That mentality was my first step in the wrong direction of parenting.

Even though Tarek was getting better, he needed to gain weight before he would be able to get discharged from the hospital. He also had to breathe on his own as well. But through maybe about a month and a half, the nurses explained that Tarek was tangling his fingers up with his breathing tube and pulling it up so they had to check him regularly to make sure he wasn't pulling on the breathing tube.

One morning as we visited Tarek, the nurse greeted us before we rounded the corner to his station. She explained the situation with the breathing tube again because he'd pulled it out in the middle of the night. A pit formed in the bottom of my stomach because I thought she was telling me that Tarek had died. She continued saying that since he'd pulled the tube out, they wanted to see if he would breathe on his own. She said excitedly that Tarek has not had his breathing tube in all night and was breathing fine on his own. Tarek had been on the breathing machine for almost two months. This was the ray of hope that everyone needed. Once his weight increased, we'd be able to go home and enjoy our son like normal.

Over time, Tarek began gaining weight and was just barely four pounds when he was discharged. As we prepared to leave the hospital, the billing office processed our insurance information. That was when we found out the total costs of the hospital stay and Tarek being on the breathing machine. It was roughly $80,000 which was a gut punch to me. *We can't win*, I thought. Our son overcame adversity, now we were stuck with a bill that would take an eternity to pay.

Come to find out, Mr. Charlie was somebody who could have been very helpful to us financially. We only spoke with him once in the two months we were there. I can't remember who gave us the information, but apparently, we should have been shown how and where to receive assistance for the bill. Charlie was supposed to be advocating for parents and facilitating information on how to proceed after leaving the hospital but instead, he spent his time chatting and flirting.

How in the hell can such a positive turn after a seeming disaster, turn back into a disaster? We remained optimistic only because we were preparing to take our son home but what average household has $80,000 just sitting around? At that time in Valdosta, you were barely going to find a job making more than $11 an hour.

What were we going to do?

3.

Back in Valdosta, we find ourselves with a new baby and a huge financial burden. When we made it home, we enjoyed everything about being new parents. Tanya and I were in a good place and we didn't even worry about the hospital bill—we didn't have the money anyways. Like most financially irresponsible people ignorant to how this burden could ruin us financially, we just chose to ignore it.

We were always tired, more so than either of us anticipated. Tanya was recovering mentally and physically. We found ourselves sleeping downstairs more often than not because we were too exhausted to walk upstairs. Many days, I would hold Tarek as long as I could. I had the tendency of holding him even until I fell asleep myself. One night in particular, I fell asleep with him lying on my stomach as I laid on the floor on my back. Tarek was only a couple of months old. I can't recall if I brought a mattress downstairs or not. I think I just made a cot out of several blankets. But I fell asleep, and when I woke up early that morning, Tarek was gone. I immediately panicked. My initial thought was that I rolled on him and flattened him like paper or something. So I jumped up and he wasn't under me. Tanya was also asleep at the time. I woke her up knowing she would panic as well, and she did.

I scanned the living room again and spotted him laying on top of my Xbox game system. I still had the game on from the night before. I don't know if he was enjoying the heat or something from the system but the biggest mystery was how did his ass scurry on top of the machine? From that point forward, I knew my son would be someone special.

When we first got home, my parents were always there lending a helping hand in any way they could. They still worked at the school, but were around Tarek any chance they got. This would set the tone for the major role they'd play in assisting with Tarek through his life. This would also be a reason that my relationship with my parents would reach a strain later, too. I have always been happy that my parents were in my life and able to help. But they never experienced the things we would soon discover.

My parents had raised their children and lived their lives already. They didn't have to play the role in Tarek's life that they did. They took it upon themselves to go above and beyond more than they should have. But two parents who grew up with nothing weren't gonna stand by and watch their son struggle with their grandchild.

Early on, my parents would help with baby supplies and even bills. I think given the financial responsibility they took to help, in some ways gave them more of a voice on things within my house and how they should be done.

Now that I'm older, I have grown to understand things

more. How could they not feel like they can dictate how somethings should be given they were technically still taking care of me in some ways, as if I was still living at home? Don't get me wrong, they weren't coming in telling me to do this and do that. But it was small subtle things I recognized at the time. Nevertheless, for the time being, I was happy they were helping.

4.

As the months passed, Tarek continued to grow. He became alert and aware of his surroundings but on the baby development scale, some things weren't happening on time. Tarek seemed to stare into space when we'd interact with him. He was putting on weight, however he was still really small for his age.

Early on, Tarek cried a lot. It wasn't a regular baby type of cry. It was a blood curdling scream most of the time. We didn't know what was going on. Tanya would cry and ask him what was wrong and eventually I grew agitated because she talked to him and asked questions as if he was going to respond. I even sometimes told her to stop talking to him like he was going to tell her what's wrong.

The doctors couldn't tell us much. They ruled out all of the most common things that babies are subjected to at that age. We were told to continue monitoring Tarek and to make sure he didn't get worse. But how would *we* know what to look for, if the doctors were saying nothing was wrong?

As time passed, things became more stressful. We didn't know what was going on with Tarek, then Tanya and I began arguing more.

The house became a reflection of what our life was turning into—it was a mess. The kitchen was always dirty, the bedrooms had clothes everywhere and baby stuff was sprawled throughout the house in every room. The diaper genie began to stink up the place. When there was cleaning being done, I was the one doing it. Tanya seemed like she was losing motivation to do much of anything.

Needing to get away, I'd go to my cousin Roy's house. Roy was like a brother growing up. He only lived across town and when we got together, we always found a way to have a good time. Going to Roy's on the weekend was an attempt to get away from the yelling, screaming, and Tanya's new dramatics. We would go to pool halls or clubs and just talk about our lives. We didn't have to go through the same issues to be able to talk. We were there for each other no matter what.

Tanya did not like me going out with Roy. She acted as if I was out galivanting or something. Most times we went out, I still respected my family enough to not be out too late. I would leave around 8PM on a Friday or Saturday night and I'd be home at 11 or 12 midnight. I never stayed out to the wee morning hours. Most clubs here weren't getting busy until 12 or 1 AM anyways. But I always made sure I didn't stay out past midnight.

One-night, Tanya waited on me to come home, like in a movie or something. It was dark inside and I shut the door and walked upstairs. I couldn't see her, but she was sitting on the couch with her legs crossed, and said, "Oh you finally decided to come home, huh?" I was confused honestly, and replied, "What are you talking about it's only 12 AM." Then that stemmed into an argument where I was being accused of creeping. I told her the truth was I wasn't, nor had ever, cheated on her and I just needed time away from everything.

I used to consult with my mom about my marital issues and my mom tried to be fair in her judgments about what people had going on. My dad normally stayed out of everybody's relationship altogether. He's not the gossiping type. But my mom attributed some of the issues we had to Tanya having postpartum depression.

Postpartum depression is commonly referred to as complications that women have after giving birth. Most cases last two to six weeks and severe or longer cases can last up to six months. I assume this may depend on what other stressors the person could have in their life. Symptoms include mood swings, anxiety, sadness, irritability, feeling overwhelmed, crying, reduced concentration, lack of concentration, etc.

I agreed with my mom once she explained the definition of postpartum. I'd never heard of such a thing. I noticed that Tanya would occasionally cry at random. Some of the symptoms seemed normal to the behavior she always had. I just chose to look past it because of being "booty blinded." So, I began to realize certain things were true about what her ex had said. The only thing that was probably normal was the fact that we had sex often, as long as we weren't arguing.

These problems grew to affect me at work as well. I became more disengaged at work—crying at times in my truck, not paying attention, and messing up delivery orders. Our issues at home were taking a toll on me. When it was time for Tanya to start back at work, we needed someone to keep Tarek. Tanya's friend, Cookie, agreed to help us. Cookie had health issues herself, but she was willing to assist us as much as she could. I would sometimes even confide in her about my marital problems.

Cookie and her husband, Samario, were a big help. He worked as a driver for sanitation services and was their only source of income. We should have chosen someone else to help because of how full their plate was at their own house. I envied their relationship. He showed her so much love and affection from what I could see. They laughed and joked constantly.

Cookie and I would occasionally talk when I would pick up Tarek. I mentioned how little Tanya did around the house and how she seemed kind of crazy in a way. Cookie knew Tanya's ex as well and explained that Tanya's ex would occasionally talk to her as well and he expressed similar stories. Cookie would never talk bad about Tanya, but she would say she saw a pattern. She thought Tanya may have grown up a certain way to cause it but the behaviors were nothing new. Cookie reminded me that I should be careful and make sure we used birth control, preventing the possibility of having another child while we were in a rough patch.

I felt kind of stupid in a way, like I was hoodwinked. But I loved Tanya, at least I think. I mean Tanya is pretty...and thick. She was down to let me make most decisions, and she had a good job. That's enough to love someone, right? I began to question my decision to marry Tanya more and more.

But I felt like I still loved her, so I was willing to try and work it out. We didn't want to continue to put stress on Cookie due to her medical problems so I decided to leave my good job and go work at a distribution center as a yard driver. The position allowed me to work Friday through Sunday and be off Monday through Thursday. Tanya made the schedule for her job and my parents could help on weekends if needed.

At this point, Tanya and I were on and off as far as mentally connecting. We were trying to work through things as best as we could. I chose to ignore a lot of things that were bothering me for what I thought was the betterment of our relationship.

Tarek was growing but his development was delayed from what I could tell. He didn't look you in the eyes until a month or so after the projected age and he wasn't able to sit up unassisted. Even making the cooing sounds that babies make was delayed. We used to sit in front of him and try to make him look at us but he would stare into space and make little noises.

Tarek was the cutest baby I'd ever seen, not bragging. His hair was extremely soft and curly and his ears poked out from the side of his head. But as he got a little older, he started keeping us up more and more through the night. The normal whine a baby makes was not how Tarek cried at all. I remember getting him to a point where he would fall asleep and I would put him down in the playpen to sleep. But he had a sixth sense or something when it came to sensing people's presence around him because he'd wake up instantly and I would hear moving around. He would make a grunting sound before letting out the most gruesome scream. It got to the point where those screams where more and more frequent. It became his typical day-to-day cry for bottles and to be changed. I became more and more agitated by his screams. In the beginning, I felt like I was doing something wrong. As time went by, I grew more and more frustrated. Tanya was bothered as well, but she was more patient than me.

5.

The screaming continued to affect me mentally. I should have sought help from anyone I could but for some reason, I thought I should handle things on my own because I didn't want anyone to see me as less of a man. How could I bring a child into this world and not be able to handle him or his screaming? Isn't that just what babies do to communicate? But I didn't realize that I was dealing with more than Tarek's behaviors. I was dealing with things in my relationship that may have been affecting how I dealt with situations.

They say it's always better to have both parents in the home but my relationship with Tanya definitely refutes that. I began reacting in frustration. I still remember the first time I exploded emotionally towards Tarek. He was maybe five or six months old and had been screaming all day. And to be clear, when I say "all day," it's not an exaggeration. He screamed at the top of his lungs incessantly. My eyes would fill with water from wanting to cry from frustration a lot of times and I'd put a pillow over my face and screamed into it.

Tanya was at work and I'd be home alone with Tarek. In frustration, I put him in the playpen hoping he would soothe himself. But he continued screaming. When I thought he couldn't get any louder, he did. I walked over to the playpen and gripped the sides in frustration and as he screamed, I screamed in his face as loudly as I possibly could. The look on his face was that of fear of not knowing what was happening. He then whimpered for a moment before screaming again.

I couldn't take it, I went to the sofa and turned the volume on the television up and tried to drown out Tarek's screams until he fell asleep. I know a lot of you may be judging me for that and it's okay. If that's the case, be warned. You will probably hate me more as you read through the rest of the book. But let me remind you, some of you have never and will never deal with some of the things between these pages. But someone is and someone needs help just as I did. This is only the beginning of me being a problem for Tarek.

Tarek's behavioral issues increased as he got older. I couldn't tell the screaming was for attention or if something was actually wrong. His pediatrician wasn't telling us anything so we assumed he was just acting out for some odd reason. Tanya grew increasingly more frustrated.

During this time, I started to let my emotions get the best of me. The screaming was nonstop. You tell me, what the fuck is a man to do in this situation?

Hmmmmm…

Then, I began to physically abuse Tarek. I'd tap his legs, only to the point where he would feel a slight sting. Assuming a baby under six months would have the common sense to figure out why he was being popped. *How fucking stupid was I? Why didn't I just call someone?*

Eventually, the pops got a bit harder and harder as time went on. So much so that Tarek's thighs became bruised and swollen. Knowing more now and reflecting back, I should never have had custody of Tarek. My mind was not in a position to take care of a child like him.

Although Tanya was on birth control, we occasionally could not be intimate because she would miss pills here and there. So, we would wait until we felt the pills were back in her system. Apparently, during one of the lapses, we ended up having sex and discovered shortly thereafter that Tanya was pregnant again. Our relationship issues were not resolved and Tarek's behavior was not improving.

All of my thoughts were directed towards what wasn't possible or even needed at that time. *We can't have another baby right now.* I was crushed. Nothing about another child felt like good news for us as a family.

Around that time, my parents retried from their jobs to help us. Tarek was growing and able to do more things like sitting up on his own. His yelling tantrums did not stop and on top of that, he started to have bowel issues. It could have been a problem all along and no one knew. I didn't know about it either. *Could I have been taking my frustrations out on him and he had physical issues happening the entire time?*

Tarek used to be extremely constipated most days. After taking him to the doctor, we were told to give him suppositories for relief. Before giving him suppositories, the doctor showed us how to relieve him, by attempting to help push out his bowel movement. We would have to dig it out as well. Tarek's butt was raw and bleeding from his bowel movements and the screams were ear-aching when cleaning him or when he was trying to pass a bowel movement. I felt like an idiot. *How could I not know this was going on with my own son?* I soften up and tried to be more caring after I was told what has happening. But then again, he'd had problems from the start. But I still didn't see it that way.

Just like in the hospital, after we got back home, I was the main person in Tarek's life. I fed, bathed, and changed him more than anyone. I don't mention that as an attempt or need to get recognition for doing my job as his parent, but I want to be clear that Tarek and I were together constantly from his birth. Of course it's easier now to recognize the strain this created. I needed someone to help because I wasn't prepared, mentally and emotionally, for what was happening. Even though I thought I was handling it well. I didn't know how to process what was going on or my feelings about my new family. I just knew life was getting exceedingly difficult and was about to get more complicated.

I began having issues at my job again. This time, the problems were occurring on and off the job. I enjoyed going to work for the most part because of some of my coworkers. I frequently sat in the security office/trucker terminal. The yard drivers as a unit would always go there to talk and joke around. I would talk mainly to the security ladies, one in particular, Denise. I knew of her and her family because they were from Lakeland, my hometown. Denise and I knew a lot of the same people so we often conversed with each other exclusively. Everyone else would talk around us. I thought Denise was attractive with a pretty smile. She laughed at all my jokes. I don't know if my liking of her was due to my marital problems or if I actually liked her. She was cool. But I knew and she knew that we couldn't talk outside of what we did at work. We never shared any explicit conversations, but I knew she knew I liked her.

My problems at work began to worsen. People started staying I wasn't working. However, when work records were pulled, they showed the opposite. The people who were doing all the talking were actually less productive than me. It didn't take long to realize that I needed a more secure job. So, I applied for a position at a prison in Florida. This job would offer better benefits and more money. I was hoping this would help make things better at home. Fingers crossed…

6.

About a year later and things were still going in the same direction as before. The only difference was my new job. My relationship with Tanya wasn't getting better, but we are making the best of the situation. While my expression of love and affection towards her didn't change because I still cared about her, her actions, and sometimes lack of action, often made me think twice about her.

After getting a new job and Tanya having the new baby (Tatyanna), we moved to a different address in the county. Tarek was a little over twelve months old and had to share his space with his baby sister. Tatyanna didn't have any complications during her birth. Tanya had to have another C-section because she had one previously with Tarek. Hindsight is always twenty-twenty. I know could have been more attentive to her mental space. I mean, I paid attention to her, but not in the way that could have helped me or her. I didn't consider the mental strain a woman could have in a two-year span with two small kids and one having special needs. Hell, Tarek was honestly too much for me to deal with mentally, so I could only imagine what may have been going through her head with all her hormones going crazy. But back then I didn't think about any of that.

I also didn't consider what Tarek could have been feeling. Most babies who have to share a space often get jealous and territorial. It's weird actually that I say this, because I never thought about it this way until I began putting it on paper.

Around this time, my mental health began fluctuating. I was up and down constantly. I definitely didn't know how to care for a special need's child, but I did what I thought everyone does. Even before Tatyanna was born, I was doing things that weren't right. I was being abusive mentally and physically towards my child because I was frustrated. I was frustrated because I had never seen or been around a child like him before. Tarek's physical behavior hadn't started yet, it was just audible annoyances for me. I could only compare it to the water bucket torture thing I heard about before. If you put a bucket near a leaky faucet, in the beginning the dripping doesn't bother you but over time, the constant sound drives you crazy. That's how I was feeling.

I know what you are thinking. How could I look at such a beautiful child in that manner? The only answer I can give is, I don't know how I got to that point. I always felt like a patient person but this was something different.

Before Tatyanna, when Tarek was close to one, I was popping him on the legs. To not hit Tarek with my hand, I had a small wooden spoon that I would use right when he started screaming. Before I did that, sometimes I would scream while pacing or while looking at him. Some days, the screaming and crying would occur all day or at a minimum, in hourlong spurts. I didn't tell anyone because I knew flat out that it wasn't right, but I justified it to myself. I knew people who would pop babies the same age for touching things they weren't supposed to or whatever. My thoughts were that it was the same thing. I just wanted him to understand so he could stop. But he never got the message and neither did I.

Tatyanna was a breath of fresh air. I wanted another boy, but she popped up. Tarek wasn't much bigger than Tatyanna. They almost looked like twins because they were the same size. Tarek wasn't walking, talking, or even crawling yet but was already one. He was very delayed. He did babble in a way though, which caused us to notice that he had a sensory disorder. He would gnaw his pacifiers like crazy. First, sucking on it and then moving it towards the side of his mouth to keep chewing. He was extremely attached to it. If you didn't give it to him or tried to get it from him, you would meet *Mr. Mayhem.*

I started working at the prison. I worked the 4 PM to 12 AM shift which worked well with Tanya's schedule. With my parents retired at the time, if we needed someone to watch the kids, they had us covered. My job was about an hour ride, one way. At times I enjoyed the ride because it gave me time to think or just clear my mind.

I would still go out every now and then with my cousin. Even though Tanya didn't say much about it, I knew it was a problem. I needed that time though. I never stopped her from doing things she wanted. I can actually say we shared the time we had with the kids equally in the beginning. In social settings, Tarek was manageable, so we would take the kids out as a family a lot.

Tatyanna progressed on schedule and as she grew, she helped Tarek progress as well. Although Tarek was older, he followed Tatyana's lead. She helped him figure out how to stand up on his own. Tarek did not learn to actually crawl until he was much older. He actually walked before he crawled. Well, more of a hop while on all fours.

When Tarek would throw tantrums, and he had many of those daily, you had to be careful because he would fling himself backwards which caused him to fall into whatever was behind him. He would play with something on the floor sitting up, he would get agitated and sling himself back whether he knew you were behind him or not. Even for such a small one year old, Tarek was extraordinarily strong. The doctor said because of him being so small at birth, he never had a chance to be in the fetal position which may be a reason he was so strong when he straightened his body. I don't know if the things the doctor told us were opinions or facts but we went with it.

That's when I started popping Tarek more. In my head, Tarek was a "normal" one year old, soon to turn two. I assumed his body may not be on schedule but his mind was fully up to speed. In a way, I was right. But in many ways, I was extremely wrong. I thought as long as I treated him in a traditional way, he'd be like Tatyanna and any other baby. In the back of my head, I knew it wasn't going to work like I wanted it to, but I was gonna try anyways.

Tarek's lungs got stronger and stronger and his screams got louder and louder. Not a regular cry but a toe-curling scream. He wasn't sleeping through the night as much as he used to and when he did sleep, he would wake up only to scream for someone to pick him up. Tanya used to cry due to Tarek constantly crying. The frustration she showed, she handled opposite of me. Tanya would pop Tarek sometimes but I was the main one using brute disciplinary tactics.

I would try to hold him for things and he would throw himself into my face and cause a headbutt. Not a small one, which still hurt, but a major one where it'd swell your ass up. Right on the lip, cheek, or the eye. There were times when Tanya and I both would be furious and throw Tarek on the sofa and walk away from him. We did not pick him up over our head or anything. But from our lap we would throw him to the sofa with him landing on his back. Now it's getting to the point where we aren't really being fully aware of how frustrated we are and what we were doing in response to the frustration.

Tarek's thighs were swollen at times from spanking his legs with the spoon. When my mother and father noticed it, they'd address it. Of course I got extremely defensive. I mean honestly how in the hell can they criticize me for something they have never experienced? I didn't want to hear anything that was in opposition to what I was doing. I would tell them Tarek is no different and has to learn just like Tatyanna. My parents always knew I was wrong and occasionally, they would voice it. I could obviously see the disappointment on their faces. I think they never really pushed the issue because they wanted to see what I was saying but they knew or thought that they couldn't do anything about it.

They were hurting knowing that their grandson was being put through what we were doing and feeling. But that pissed me off more because what about me? What about the stuff I was going through. I was going crazy obviously. Why didn't they see my pain?

Are the tantrums for attention? Are they because he really doesn't know what he's doing? Is he trying to hit me in the face when he jumps back, hitting me in the face? These are the questions I asked myself when I got mad. I would start pacing the floor like a mad man. I began enjoying going to work because it was an escape from home.

The house was always a mess. Tatyana's room had her crib in it and a dresser. But we threw clothes and everything in there, even with her sleeping in the crib. We were messed up in the head, whether we showed it or not. I think we played it off well to people outside of the home besides my parents. Tarek's room was probably the cleanest of all because it wasn't much in it from the beginning.

Most kids with siblings always fight and hit, even at a young age. Tarek started to hit around the time both he and Tatyanna began to stand and walk. Tatyanna was closer to a year old. Tarek would frequently grab her hair when she would get close to him. Sometimes Tarek would even reach to scratch her face. Some people may say that's what kids that age do. That may be so, but over time, it became much more frequent.

To recall certain events better as I write these words, I

had my mother send some of Tarek's baby pictures. When Tanya and I split, which will be discussed later, she took all of Tarek's pictures and gave me a small envelope worth of them. Looking back through the pictures, I became emotional. It was such a difficult time. Seeing how innocent and beautiful he looked in the pictures made me want to throw up at the thought of what he was going through, especially since aspects of it were from me. Tears fall as I type this but I hope my experience keeps someone else from committing the same mistakes as me and feeling the way I feel now.

7.

In 2009, Tarek began "self-stimulating himself." I think that is what it is called. Arm flapping and noises while doing it. You can tell things were different because he even laughed differently. No snickering or typical laughter but more of screeching as a way of him laughing. If Tatyanna had a pacifier, Tarek would have his. He seemed as if he needed it more than most kids. This seemed to be a form of stimulation as well. He would just gnaw all day and hum while doing it. We would go through multiple pacifiers because after he grew his teeth, he began to bite through the pacifier nipple.

At the age of three, Tarek began going to physical, speech, and occupational therapy. Mr. Frank was his physical and occupational therapist. He was like an extended father that I needed on my side. Of course, Frank didn't know the things that were going on in our home. But in his methods, he was very stern. Tarek never acted out much with Frank, even until this day. Frank suggested we try the tubing from fish tanks for Tarek to chew on instead of pacifiers because they were more durable. Those worked great. Tarek loved them, they lasted a long time, and they soothed him for a little bit during the day.

Tatyanna was only two but she began understanding that she needed to maintain safe distances from Tarek, at times. Tatyanna loved to be around Tarek. She mocked his actions not knowing that Tarek was also attempting to mimic her progress too. Tarek would occasionally become aggressive with Tatyanna, until we as parents tried to raise her to give him space. He would hit, slap, or scratch her or anyone else out of nowhere at any time for any reason.

We began trying to teach Tarek to be more independent. He'd sometimes lie in the bed in his room watching movies on repeat all day. Because before we did repeat, we learned that certain things would trigger his tantrums. Most of the time, we wanted to be two steps ahead of him. He would often watch a few select animated movies, but as soon as they ended, mayhem ensued. Tarek would knock the TV over, try to pull out drawers (small ones), or throw clothes all over the floor until someone finally turned the movie back on. Although as parents, we didn't want to reinforce the negative behavior, we had to make a choice. Was it worse to play a movie over and over again or deal with the mayhem?

I'll take peace for $200, Alex!

Trying to get Tarek used to his own room was hell on wheels. This was no doubt our fault. We tried to baby him in the beginning while hoping for peace, by letting him lay in the bed with us. That made it more difficult for him to transition to his own room. We started out small. I would try to put him to sleep and then place him in his room. But the instant I put him down on the bed, he'd pop up and what do you think happened next? You guessed it! A combination of screaming, biting, and scratching because of fighting sleep. Some parents allow children to self-soothe by putting them in their room and allowing them to cry themselves to sleep. Tanya and I tried to block Tarek in his room with a dog/baby gate in the doorway. Tarek would literally stand in the doorway and scream and cry until one of us would come. If we did not come, he would stand there all night. I don't mean that figuratively. Literally, ALL NIGHT!

This was also the beginning of Tarek's self-injurious behaviors. He would scratch his face and bang his head on walls or tables. His fingers were like razor blades. He would scratch his face revealing the next layer of skin. You could not leave him upset for long. If you did not matter where you were—bathroom or whatever—when you came back, he would be bleeding from scratching himself.

The first time I noticed Tarek bang his head or scratch himself, he was watching TV and got upset about something. I cannot tell you exactly what it was, but he yelled and then slammed his head into the table. When he was smaller, he would lightly tap his heads on the table, but I never thought he would get to the point where I thought he would break our table.

This is where I hoped ABA therapy would help him early on. Tarek received ABA therapy from Dr. Baker Wright out of Tallahassee, Florida. The therapists that would come up were young, like college kids. But I wouldn't have changed those therapists for anything. They would come in to the home and allow me to go get Tatyanna from daycare or go the store. I never worried about them doing anything to harm Tarek. They were everything I wasn't to him. They were patient and understood him and his needs. Tarek's occupational therapist, Frank, was the same way.

8.

Because of Tarek's age and delays, he was able to start school with a special Pre-K program at three years old. Tarek's teachers were very warm and nice. They cared a lot about the kids that were in their class. I felt comfortable and relieved that Tarek would be attending school. I thought it would be a good chance for me to get some rest when at home. I can't lie, I looked at the situation like, "He's their problem now!" I wasn't even leaving Tarek there all day, only a few hours which was to eventually get him used to the thought of being at school all day.

Not long after beginning, Tarek began having issues at school. He frequently bit and scratched other children while they slept. While I tried to enjoy my time alone, it would soon come to a halt due to behaviors the school could not handle. I began picking up Tarek early from school because his behaviors weren't manageable for the teachers. It would either be his aggressive disruptions or the constant screaming and yelling in class.

This became almost an everyday occurrence. It would even come to problems on the school bus because Tarek was being disruptive. His teachers refused to give up on him.

They would continue to let Tarek come back to school every day. Of course, I knew why he was being sent home because I was dealing with the same things at home. It was aggravating because I had to get him early, because the professionals couldn't do what I had to do all day.

Eventually the teacher would regret to inform us that Tarek was having too many problems and was becoming a distraction to the rest of the kids in the classroom. I wasn't as upset as I thought I would be. It was just my evidence that there was an apparent problem that no one was addressing.

The teachers told us about a school for kids with behavioral problems. The school was for kids with special needs to address and work on the behavioral issues and eventually be placed back in to the regular classroom setting.

Personally, I was loving the idea. I grew up in that area and had never heard of the school or program but I thought it was dope. I hoped the things Tarek and I would learn would make a difference at home. It still hurt to think that even at three years old, Tarek didn't make it through a regular school year without being placed in a special program.

After visiting the school for Tarek and meeting his new teacher, Betty, I was shocked to find out the new school for my son was actually an old elementary school that was shared between the Academy and the alternative school students. For those of you who don't understand this dynamic, the alternative schools in Georgia are for "normal" kids who have issues in regular school and can't go back. I didn't realize it then so much, but I don't understand who thought coupling these two very different groups of children was a good idea. You take small children with disabilities and special needs and place them in a building where they can see and model behaviors exhibited by "delinquent" kids. This in itself is counterproductive from the start.

I had a bad feeling about this but what could I do about it? I needed time to myself and school was the perfect time and place to make that happen.

Right? Wrong.

Tarek began having the same issues as he'd had at his prior school. Given the recommendation to move to this new academy, I assumed his behavior was expected and prepared for by the staff. Unfortunately, that was far from true. At the time, they only had two teachers in the classroom. It may have been five students in the class, but I knew Tarek was going to call for a lot of attention.

Just like at his other school, Tarek became aggressive towards other kids in the classroom. Now remember that this is the school that is supposed to have help for his behavior. At that time, Tarek was only receiving speech and occupational therapy in school for one day per week. This is someone with extensive speech delays and behavioral issues. Tarek could barely grasp and secure objects in his hands. But to be in a behavioral school and not be receiving extensive behavioral therapy was beyond comprehension to me. The academy soon began calling me to pick up Tarek early from school and he was still going for only half a day. I even had to pick him up from the school bus at times, because drivers and monitors weren't supplied with proper seating equipment for children like Tarek.

At this point, I did not have a clue of what steps to take. I didn't know what Tarek's rights were as a student and mine as a parent. Technically, I still don't currently. The little hope I did have for space and/or help began slowly dwindling away. Tanya worked during the day. So, whenever Tarek and Tatyanna needed to be picked up, it was my responsibility.

We both would get up in the middle of the night but a lot of times, it was me doing the most to get him to bed which began affecting my job performance. Up all night, then picking the kids up usually after only an hour or two of Tarek at school, then go home for a few hours and not sleep. Then pick up Tatyanna from daycare. While wanting to lay in the bed, it was then time to get ready for work. My parents would be there until Tanya got home. I thought things couldn't get any worse.

My conflicts with Tarek's education and the academy continued for years into the present day. The school's biggest problem with Tarek has been them pacifying his behavior. They have done this so much they did not know how to actually deal with him or identify professionals who could help him.

I expressed that I would like Tarek's ABA therapists to come to the school and assist with him but—DENIED!

I expressed that Tarek needs a one on one person to assist him—DENIED!

I suggested that the school find a more satiable school for Tarek—DENIED!

The school pretty much informed me that it wasn't extreme enough yet. My mother, a retired educator, explained that those decisions were about not wanting to spend the money. Why else would they deny his obvious needs for services? Instead, the school continued to bribe Tarek with food and trips to the gymnasium to keep him calm through the day.

Even recently, I have had IEP meetings where the speech therapist treats Tarek once a week. She spoke about his goals not being met and she did not see a reason for his appointments to increase. She eventually admitted to not increasing his time because of his behavior. They continue not to serve my son based on his disability. I still pick Tarek up from school because of his behavior and continue to be threatened that Tarek will face suspension because of his behavior.

Most people complain about simple school problems like grades for the nine weeks, bus arrangements, student affairs, etc. I have had a ten-year battle with a school that is supposed to specialize in behavioral intervention. I still battle with getting Tarek the minimal amount of services beyond the standard student. This is the same school system that is being sued for misplacing special needs kids and not giving them the same opportunities they are required to receive.

In the past year, in a two-month span, Tarek was physically restrained over forty times. So imagine the entire year and times they may not have reported. Think about the children that are constantly being hurt by Tarek. The teachers don't even want to be around him. His teachers change every year. I've had someone tell me who works with at academy say that Tarek runs all the teachers off because they can't deal with him. Good school, huh?!?

9.

Working at any prison can be mentally draining. I worked at a low-level security prison but it still had some violent offenders. Doesn't matter the level of the inmates, the job itself is still stressful. It's like a big daycare for adults with adult problems.

I actually loved being a correctional officer. You learn that inmates are just people with rough pasts, who might not have received enough resources or attention to overcome certain obstacles. On the other hand, I have also met some psychopaths.

When Tarek started school, things were difficult for me mentally. Every day was a torture session for me. I never looked forward to not waking up until then. Aside from him, Tanya and I were always off and on. I would constantly get mad because it seemed like Tanya lacked motivation to do anything. You know just like young girls, men have an idea of what they feel a wife is and does in the relationship. But I found myself doing a lot of things I thought she would enjoy doing. I'm not trying to come off as a chauvinist. I don't think women have a specific place, but I was raised watching the mother cook every day for the family. But with

Tanya, we ate out a lot. If we weren't eating out, I cooked more than I wanted to cook. She might disagree and this isn't to slander who Tanya is or used to be, but I want you to understand certain parts of my life and how it may have influenced my decisions.

As far as the cleaning, I can't lie. There was barely any cleaning done. It wasn't terrible inside the house but toys were everywhere. The rooms were a little messy, but the front room would make you second guess sitting down. It was to a point with Tanya that I looked at her as just a sexual object because I didn't like being with her anymore. But I couldn't leave her because I had two kids with her and as soon as I'd try to leave, she would put me on child support. Maybe if I stayed, things would change. In hindsight, she could have easily been coping with her own depression or unhappiness.

I began gaining weight like crazy. At my heaviest, I was up to 350lbs. I was so miserable, I could feel the anxiety in my chest. I hated going home. Everything she did frustrated me. I didn't even like to hear her "baby talk" voice or laugh. On a scale of irritability between one and ten, I was probably at a seventeen.

When we went to the doctor's office to get Tarek's behaviors and restlessness checked, she would tell what she thought were innocent lies. She wanted to appear as if Tarek was progressing when he wasn't. Maybe she thought it made us look better as parents. But in my frustrations, I would begin to call her out during the appointments. I could have chosen better ways to address my frustration but at the time,

I dealt with it as best as I knew how.

We took Tarek to a neurologist. He gave Tarek a sedative that he said would normally put a grown man to sleep for hours. Tarek slept for twenty minutes before waking up during the test. I had to hold him because when he got antsy, he also got moody. Over time, I began quelling some of his antsy behavior by squeezing him on the inner thigh. It was one of those pinches your grandparents would give you when you were moving around too much in church as a child. It was subtle but effective. Well, at least for "regular" kids it could be. I made it a regular way to control Tarek. When he started having fits, I would put him in my lap and pinch him when I felt he needed it, which was too damn much. But I thought it was less abrasive than grabbing him. At times, Tanya would spank Tarek, too. However, she would get upset and I always felt like I could put an end to it better than she could. So I found myself trying to be the main disciplinarian and person to deal with Tarek.

I couldn't get help from anyone because no one understood how to deal with him. All anyone did was pass judgment. *Derek you shouldn't be doing this, you shouldn't be doing that.* Blah, blah, blah. But nobody was lining up to come and get him to see if they could do better. If they believed they could do better, take him. Let's see.

My parents would often confront me and we'd argue. They had every right to confront me about what I was doing. They wanted the best for me, but more for my kids. I wasn't willing to accept criticism from anyone who didn't feel or understand how I felt. My relationship with my dad started to fracture. On occasions, I'd remind him that I was the head of my house and I could do as I pleased. I failed to recognize that I was behaving like a horrible excuse for a father and man.

My parents spoiled Tarek and Tatyanna which was a blessing. But I thought it was becoming counterproductive for Tarek. Even though he wasn't diagnosed with autism until the age of five, he has always been a creature of habit. He would watch the same movies a thousand times. All he wanted to eat was bread, tortillas, pancakes, and fries—anything high in starch.

Over time, he learned that when he cried around my parents, he would be rewarded by being given something because they didn't want to see him cry or be upset. My parents were passionate about them being taken care of, but I hated what I thought it was doing to Tarek. When I expressed my concern, it was never received or considered. But I needed my parents. They were always there, even though I didn't want them to be sometimes.

Then I had the school calling when I was trying to rest. My days off were typically during the week. So I would only get about two hours away from Tarek during my day of rest from work. I grew more and more aggravated and emphasized to the school that I needed him to be there so I could have a break. What those teachers were struggling to deal with for two hours, I was managing alone some days and I was mentally exhausted.

I had to drive through Clyattville, Georgia, to Madison for work. My route included crossing a bridge right before entering Pinetta (Madison County), Florida. Almost instantly, I would visualize what it would be like to drive my car into the river. My biggest fear is drowning though. I would one day pull over to the side of the rode before the bridge and seriously consider running into the water, knowing there was a good chance I wouldn't be able to escape and swim to the bank. I wanted to die but I didn't want to be tortured in the process. I wanted it quick. I began looking at the trees while riding by. So I started visualizing running into a tree nearby and how quickly I could get it over and done with.

I didn't want to continue going through life as it was, but I was punking out from just killing myself and escaping the mental anguish. I never thought about suicide with anyone in the car with me. I guess I felt if I died, my spirit would be at peace by itself.

I can't remember who told me to see a psychiatrist, but after thinking about it for a while, I finally went. I told him everything I was going through and thinking. He told me what I already knew. I was suffering from depression to the 10th power. He prescribed me with an extremely high dose of Xanax. I only took it for about a month, maybe two. I did not give a damn about what was going on around me when I was taking those pills. Someone could've tried to attack me and I probably wouldn't have moved or cared.

Tarek seemed like he could tell something was different. I remember him "turning up" the behaviors to get my attention. He started bouncing on the bed and throwing himself over the side. I caught him one or two times and then I just told him, "When your ass kisses that floor, I bet you'll sit down somewhere."

As I lounged across the bed, he kicked and screamed and I didn't even care. I would finally be at peace in my head and the behaviors didn't bother me. Tarek, as a last resort, flung himself off the bed and hit the floor hard. I got up and walked to the kitchen with him screaming and hopping after me.

The only reason I stopped taking the meds was because everybody kept telling me they didn't like the change in who I was when I was on them. People are never satisfied. First, I was too hard and angry. Then I was too out of touch with reality. Regardless, I didn't like having to go to the doctor so often, I just wanted the damn meds so I could be on my way. But I soon came off of them and was back to stressing again.

10.

By the time Tarek reached four and five years old, we were experimenting with different medicines to help stabilize his mood swings and tantrums. He was finally diagnosed with autism and with the diagnosis, we hoped it would create more opportunities for assistance. I also hoped the school would figure something out. Tarek was still behaving the same way at home and at school.

With my mom working in a school system for thirty years, her expertise made me aware of many different options and things that should be available to us as parents. I began having my mom advocate for Tarek in school since she knew a lot more than I did.

To be pacified at school, the teachers and administration began doing things for Tarek beyond what I expected them to do. Tarek needed help not to be contained for the day. We began to complain about him not being at school the whole day and asking the school about letting Dr. Wright come into the school and help. It was counterproductive to have therapy at home where certain methods were taught but at school he ran wild.

Tarek was tearing up the classroom and attacking

students and teachers on a daily basis. Betty, Tarek's teacher, would have the teacher's aide go to a local fast-food restaurant to get Tarek nuggets to calm him in times of breakdowns. I would even come to the school and they would tell me the only way they could get him to calm down was to take him to the cafeteria to get some popsicles. Tarek may have had issues with displaying certain emotions, however, he still knew how to play off people's emotions.

Because I was hardest on Tarek, of course he was on his best behavior with me, if there was such a thing. No one else could control him as much as I could. But my control was based on spankings and outbursts.

I asked the school leadership what they planned to do about his problems in the classroom. The school downplayed the behavior in the IEP meetings, but would call me daily or tell me about his breakdowns. I was told about the parents complaining about their kids being bit and scratched and coming home with new marks.

As a parent, I felt bad and ashamed but I needed help that the school system wasn't willing to give. They never said it, but they knew any extra help needed during school hours would have to be facilitated by them. My mom explained that schools get special funding from the state for special needs programs and often, the money is used to fund other programs in the school. For instance, the program Tarek was in was only designed to be a short-term program to get the kids back into the regular classroom. Not to spoil the ending but Tarek hasn't returned to the "regular" classroom even as I type.

My mom told me about a situation happening to a family I knew as a child. The woman's child was deaf. Because the school did not have the resources to teach or manage the child's disability, the child was sent to a school for the deaf in Alabama. The enabled the child to have the same opportunities to learn and function like his brother and sister back home. So, I assumed Tarek's school would probably need to set up the same arrangements because he was too much for everyone at that school. Needless to say, that never happened. When it was brought up during the meetings, the idea would be dismissed as if there wasn't a need for it.

Parents of disabled children need more avenues to discuss problems. We need assistance fighting school systems who are forgetting about our children. We see how funds are spent and what's prioritized. You mean to tell me the football team can get new uniforms every year, but my son can't get the opportunity to be "normal" in some other school because no one wants to pay for it?

That's some bullshit!

And I'd call them on their bullshit! But That's all I knew to do. The administration became highly agitated with my mother and I because we pushed for more. We never got anything beneficial except different teachers every year because they couldn't deal with my son. No one ever said that but you could tell the affect Tarek had on the school itself. The children in the alternative school knew Tarek by name. Male workers were often called to assist during his outbursts and they weren't even working for the Horizon program! They would take him to the gym, just so he would be able to find something to do.

When I'd run into people in public or at the store, they'd speak to Tarek and ask me if he was my son. When I confirmed, their expression would switch to a mix of concern and pity. I knew what they were thinking because a lot of times, I was thinking the same thing. Tarek was a local celebrity because of his aggressive behavior. But the school still wouldn't let Dr. Wright's ABA group come into the classroom and help with Tarek.

I bet some of you probably think I am exaggerating the story a bit but I'm really not. These events are imprinted in my head because of the overall impact they've had on my life. It hurts knowing that people can see you're hurting at home, and call you to relieve them of a temporary issue and they have the responsibility and resources to help themselves.

I knew it was going to be a long road ahead but I never would have guessed there would be little to no help. Thus far, the only program that's been helpful has been Easter Seals. The program was great. They provided travel assistance for going long distances to and from Tarek's appointments. They would send a supply of baby wipes and diapers. Because even at school age, Tarek was still using diapers and training pants. Easter Seals would eventually offer respite care to us as well.

11.

By 2010, I was tired of the school, frustrated because of work, my relationship was in shambles, and Tarek was still behaving per usual. All this combined became too much to handle. Around that time, I discovered Facebook. I created a profile with no real goal because I honestly didn't know what it was all about. But one day, I received a friend request from a former colleague—Denise.

Of course I accepted but I think I messaged her first and asked how she was doing. I looked at her page and saw she had a man and a daughter. I still didn't think anything of the situation. We both agreed that it would be nice to see each other and we decided to meet.

Like some weirdos, we met up in a mass retailer's parking lot. When she got out of the car, she looked like she hadn't changed a bit. Same nice smile and all. We laughed and talked for a bit then we opened up about our past feelings. We told each other that we really liked one another back then and were happy to see each other now.

She told me she and her boyfriend were having issues. Of course I told her about certain stress I was dealing with as well. I don't know about her, but I needed whatever this relationship was going to be. I needed a break from home. I needed a break from what my life had become. I needed something different.

It's no surprise but our connection and openness led to us sleeping together. Our affair started out at a hotel but then we figured, *why spend money*. Instead, we'd meet anywhere—a park, empty parking lot, wherever. Denise was just what I needed. I could talk to her about any and everything and she never passed judgement. She never said too much, but she always said just enough. Denise treated me as a king on an intimate level, to where it was things I never had to ask for.

The only bad thing about what we had was the fact that both of us had other lives outside of the moments we spent together. Our kids were about the same age and they would never be able to play together.

On weekends, I would tell Tanya I was going to my cousin's house. For the most part, it was true. I would go to Roy's house for a moment and talk, then Denise and I would meet up. It didn't matter where we went as long as we were together. Tanya eventually became suspicious of everything, but she couldn't prove it and I damn sure wasn't admitting it. This is my first open admittance to cheating on Tanya. I got tired of coming home to the same ol, same ol. When I left home, things were a mess and when I came home, things were still a mess. I got tired of saying the same thing constantly to her. I would tell her things weren't working out, but I would never leave. I didn't leave because of guilt or anything. I was afraid of what child support would do to me financially and just the unknown, period.

I knew of some people who stayed together until their kids were adults and they split right after, I just didn't know if I should do it or wait. I knew Denise would be there if I left because she had already told me many times. I truly cared about Denise, but could some of that have been due to the circumstances? Given the void I had in my life, Denise was becoming the spark I needed to keep going.

I regret how I handled things. I was confused on where my life was headed and which steps to take. I may not have liked Tanya, but I still loved her. Although I was attracted to her physically, there didn't seem to be any mental stimulation between us. As I grew, I needed more of something, that I wasn't getting in my marriage.

Eventually, I started visiting Denise at her apartment. She had apparently broken up with her boyfriend and professed her love for me. It didn't matter to her that I was still married, she was down for me. But I couldn't do the same for her just yet and she was ok with that.

Denise made me feel welcomed and appreciated, I taught her how to make certain meals and I did things for her, no one else has done before. We bought gifts for each other, the whole nine. I was living like I had another family.

Even during this time, I never neglected to take care of the kids. I was there most of time with Tarek. I'd been working the night shift at the prison which gave me more time to do things with the kids during the day, so we wouldn't have to have much help with child care. My kids always came first, but I put Denise before Tanya in a way. I spent more time with Tanya at home but I wanted to be elsewhere.

Denise and I would meet in a dark parking lot in front of a distribution center almost every night before I went to work. I would leave early by at least an hour to make time for whatever we were going to do. Some days we would just sit and talk. Some days we did much more.

At one point, Denise and I stopped seeing each other. Our conversations were always genuine. I told her I didn't know how to leave Tanya and I didn't think it was fair to Denise to drag her along. Although she didn't want to do it, she agreed to take a break.

During our time apart, I tried to make things right with Tanya to see if we really could make things better between us. I still thought of Denise but I wasn't ready to leave my family. It didn't take long for me to figure out that things were never going to change. Not long after, I went back to speaking with Denise and we began to see each other once again only to break up later for the same reason.

Tanya actually knew more than I thought. She would snoop around in my car. One time she told me she noticed small footprints on my windshield. She was probably going through my phone at one point but I stopped caring.

I think Tanya had my speakers stolen later, too. One night I came home from actually hanging out with my cousin and I got out of my 2005 Cadillac Deville and looked back at the car to make sure the trunk was closed and nothing was on inside the car. I hit the horn, went inside, and laid down. Tanya woke me up in the middle of the night, and was like, "I don't know if your trunk was open or not, but I think somebody stole your speakers." I got up went outside, looked into the trunk and saw my speakers were missing. I closed the trunk like they were still there, walked back into the house and laid back in the bed without getting upset. I knew she had something to do with it but I didn't even care. Call it karma I guess.

12.

Skipping ahead a couple years, I can go on and on about the everyday struggles with Tarek. While you may not get an accurate depiction of his constant behavioral issues, just know his breakdowns were frequent. We finally found a medication that slowed Tarek down to where I was at peace. No one else liked it. I guess everyone else always wants to tell you how things and people should be in your house, even though they have limited experience dealing with it. My family communicated that they didn't like Tarek on the medication because he didn't seem like himself. But wasn't that the whole point? Not to make him lethargic, but to slow him down to where he could function normally.

During the time where he was on the meds, he was super chill which made me happy because I could take him out and do things without having to worry about a breakdown. I could think and wouldn't have to be so rough with him. But of course, everyone else knew best and wanted him off of the meds.

Tanya seemed like she may not have liked the guilt from the comments that were made, so she pretty much went along with what others said. Tarek came off the meds and cranked back up not soon after.

Looking back over the next couple of years, I can actually say I didn't spank Tarek often, I beat him. I felt like a robot at times. It became more of an automatic reaction and Tarek knew it was coming just from screaming out. He recognized the clinks of the belt buckle as I walked towards him or into the room. If he was at the beginning of an outburst, I would pick up the belt and shake it just to scare him when I was tired or felt guilty for constantly beating him.

Using a belt meant leaving marks which were on his back, legs…wherever. I lied to family and whoever asked questions because I knew it was cowardly and I was ashamed. Tarek also began taking his self-injurious behavior to a different level. He scratched himself more and more. Always having scabs and marks on his face and head. Whenever he got upset, he whined and scratched himself. Even if it was because a movie went off or the weather was bad. He began head banging anything.

I left him in his room one day because he wouldn't stop screaming and yelling. I put him in his room to keep myself from hurting him and closed his door. Moments later, he banged his head into the door and the wall with so much force, he made small indentions. Out of frustration in seeing the damage, along with his constant screaming, I grabbed him and thrust him into the wall creating a bigger hole. I got so angry with myself for constantly responding to his behavior with my negative behavior. But no one would take him. I constantly argued with my dad to take him if he thought he could do better, but he never did. My thoughts were, if you're not going to help or take him, keep that shit to yourself. I don't want to hear what I'm doing wrong and you ain't doing shit to help. Even when Tarek would act up, my parents would use me as a scare tactic.

"You better stop or I'm going to tell your daddy." So this, in an indirect way, made me think what I did was ok, it's just nobody else wanted to do it. So I had to be the bad guy to better him. Because whenever something went on, I was always the one that was called to get Tarek together.

Tarek had gotten bigger and stronger. He was behind on the size scale for his age group but Tarek was a natural brute. He'd knock things over in the house which sent me into rages. He pulled drawers out of the dressers and throw the clothes everywhere, he knocked over the dresser with the TV, he knocked lamps down, and whatever else he could get his hands on or kick. Could Tarek have been responding to the things I was doing from the beginning? Possibly, but I was too far gone myself to even realize it and know how to fix it.

Around 2012, I lost my job at the prison. I was dismissed due to not being able to perform my duties as a correctional officer. Of course the reasons run deeper than what others know. But my complications with sleep had come from the challenges of my son and my health in general.

Tarek was up all night almost every night. If he would go to bed at 9 PM, he would wake up at 11 PM and be up until 5 AM, if he even went back to sleep. Many days, I was left with no sleep. I got up with him majority of the times because I was the only person who had some control over him. So when I went to work at night, I started falling asleep on post, whether it was in the dorm or in the truck that drove around the perimeter of the prison.

Because my sleep was so disturbed, I began having night terrors more and more. This is no exaggeration, I found it hard to distinguish reality from dreams because I could fall asleep so easily. One time in particular, I was in the perimeter truck and I had a dream that I'd dosed off. The road around the perimeter is sloped towards the ditch. In my dream, I was riding the slope around the prison only to end up hitting a post at the corner and totaling the truck. This was real as hell. I could feel the bumps and smell the air, only for me to wake up and I was sitting at the gas pumps near the gate and had no clue how I got there or how long I had been there.

Another time, I was in the dorm and it was lights out. A few inmates were still walking around the open bay dorm going to the bathroom and fixing soups heading back to their bunks. I remember a few of the inmates standing in front of me and one of them growing wings and flying out of the dayroom into the ceiling. Next thing I know, an inmate was tapping on the window to the bubble I was in. He was laughing and said, "Aye big homie, you good?" I laughed it off, but he would have never understood why I was like that.

After many incidents, I asked to be moved to day shift. I had other problems on day shift that I won't go into. But the biggest memory that I had was a conversation with an inmate in the confinement/life dorm. That was where more violent people were on the compound. I got respect from pretty much all inmates because I treated them like men until they treated me otherwise. But one conversation in particular hit me the hardest. It was football season and I was standing in the dayroom amongst the inmates and I was talking to one of the older guys from Ft. Lauderdale. I can't remember his name, but he loved FSU and I am a Miami fan. But I normally never talked about my family situation, but for some reason that day, I confided in him. I explained the situation with my son and how he can be in public and how people look when we are out. In so many words, he told me he wouldn't give a damn what anyone thought, he would take his son wherever and dare anyone to say anything or he would curse their ass out. I looked at him and thought about what he said to me. Only to later use his tactics on a regular basis.

I was unemployed for about a year or so and looking for work. I was depressed about issues from my old job and I was left with Tarek at home whenever he was there. I was scared for the both of us. I did small jobs like drive school buses for a couple of months. I learned quickly that I may have had PTSD, because those kids thought I was crazy.

I couldn't put my hands on them but I would stop that damn bus on the side of the road and cut it off because I wanted peace and quiet riding down the road. My expectations may have been too high. But I figured these are "regular" kids and they should know better and listen when they are told something the first time. I eventually left from driving for the school because I could not do it mentally.

By this point, Tanya and I were pretty much done with each other. We were just cohabitating. We had intimate moments but afterwards, would barely talk to each other. I was ready to go, but didn't know how to leave. Tanya began going out more and doing things. I didn't know where she was going sometimes, and I didn't really care. I can't lie though, a couple of times she went out and dressed up for the club or something. She looked good, I can't hate. But I wanted more than that in my relationship.

I don't remember why, but one day Tanya was walking around singing R&B love/hate songs. She had a baseball and was singing the lyrics, "I'll bust the windows out your car!" I cursed her out and told her to go right ahead and her ass was gonna pay for it, since the car was in her name too.

The only reason I was ever written up at work was because of Tanya. Both of our checks go into the same account. So one day, I got to the gas pump after just getting paid. I needed gas to drive to work. My card was declined multiple times. I called in to work and explained that I could not come because I didn't have access to my money for gas. I took a picture and everything in uniform.

The next day, I called the bank because the notification said the card was stolen or something. Come to find out, Tanya cancelled my card to the account that our money went to because she was angry. I may have done some immature things in my day, but none of them would affect someone's money or career. For me, that was the last straw.

Tatyanna was growing, but unfortunately, she played the background a lot of the time. Things that Tatyanna needed in younger social crowds, she didn't get because she was home around me and Tarek. Another thing that frustrated me with Tanya was when Tatyanna was in kindergarten, Tanya was often headed to work and never did Tatyana's hair for school. Tatyanna had nice textured, but thick, hair. For a man like myself, I didn't know what the hell to do. So I learned the proper way to put Tatyana's hair into a ponytail. I would occasionally practice trying to braid her hair on occasions too. I was never brave enough to put a braid in it and send her to school though. I used to ask Tatyanna's teachers or any Black females I saw walk into the school if my ponytails were acceptable. Most of the women I asked were shocked and looked at me with surprise in their eyes that I was doing my daughter's hair. Little did they know, I had to in order to keep her from looking like a chia pet.

I feel bad for Tatyanna. She lacked attention for so many years because we had to devote a lot of time to Tarek. Tatyanna was always taken care of and was given her own time, but it was nowhere close to the time and attention that Tarek received. I hope when she gets to the age where she understands, she will know that I wanted to spend just as much time with her, I just couldn't. My relationship with Tatyanna would never grow to where it should be in my eyes. I wish I could have done a lot of things differently.

I got to a point where I didn't want to be confined to the house. Whether it was just Tarek and I, or if Tatyanna went too, we went to more places together. Tarek still had his moments but I decided to take the advice I'd gotten at the prison. We went to the store, the park, etc. People complimented me for having such well-behaved children ad I thought, *You have no idea.*

By this time, Tarek was around seven years old and had three different teachers at the Horizon Academy. At school his behavior worsened. I think he knew they would call me from school. Tarek would torment other kids in the class, especially when they took naps. That was primarily when he became aggressive towards them. Even after being at the Academy for four years, nothing had changed. They had not sought any behavioral help and had not implemented a change to their teaching method. Only thing that changed was that they kept him for the entire day of school, from 8 AM to 1:30 PM. Then he'd sit there until the bus came around 2 PM to take him home. If Tarek would so much as coughed during school, they would send him home because they would say he was sick. For the slightest thing, I would be called. We would eventually call them out on a lot of things that were happening and my relationship soured with the Academy's administration.

After the bus driving job, I worked security at a bank for a few months. Tanya and I had decided to separate. We continued living together until we figured something out. I had it my head that we were done, so of course I didn't wait or give myself time to let things settle. I didn't consider Tanya or what she was feeling, all I knew was that she agreed to proceeding with a divorce and that was all I cared about at the time.

I began scrolling some of the dating sites looking for something to do. I really wasn't interested in a relationship honestly. I don't even know why I didn't call Denise. She would have normally been my first choice. I was all over the damn place. I know I didn't want Denise to deal with the troubles I was having at home. I was nervous about that. I thought that Tarek might change my relationship with her.

After scrolling a dating app around New Year's Day, I came across the profile of a gorgeous chick. I knew she was out of my league so I just looked at her pics and kept scrolling. Later, I received a message from her just saying hi. I was shocked but replied. Her name was Tasheena. We continued talking and grew a little closer through our conversation. Eventually, I told her about my situation with Tanya. I should have said something in the beginning but I feared my honesty would abruptly end the conversation. I knew I hadn't told her about Tanya but I played like I simply couldn't remember. She called me out on not telling her about my current living situation, so I thought that was the end of that.

13.

Tasheena texted me a day later explaining the importance of being real with her. From then on, we talked often. After agreeing to meet, she gave me her address. I was extremely nervous. She was in the Air Force and had her own house. It was big and nice as hell.

The first time I saw her, I thought, *Oh my! Damn! As* we talked, she kinda played a shy Janet Jackson type of role. She went and put on a fresh ponytail out the closet. She was dressed comfortably in sweats and t-shirt but dolled up at the same time. We had good conversation. We eventually went out a couple of times. Even at this point, I never thought we would get into a relationship. She was far beyond what I felt was in my range. Besides, I still was living with Tanya.

I told Tanya that I was talking to Tasheena and that Tasheena was just a friend. I told her Tasheena wanted Tatyanna to come play with her daughter, Alita. Tanya didn't take that well. I didn't think Tasheena would want to be with me, but if she did, I would most definitely have taken her up on it.

Tanya agreed for me to take Tatyanna to play with

Alita. The first time they met, Tatyanna was around five or six, shy, and didn't talk much. Tasheena felt it would be a good idea for the kids to see us interact with each other since we were having these play dates. So we all agreed to meet and have a play date at the park. I don't think Tanya ever took the kids to the park much by herself. Tasheena and I dressed comfortably, like any normal parents would. I had the kids with me and when Tanya showed up, she had on a green sweater, jeans and boots with a skinny heel.

To a park….

For a play date...with children…

Because this park, like most, has soft turf under the equipment so kids won't hurt themselves, heels puncture the foam. I do not know what Tanya was thinking when she got dressed but it did not make any sense to me.

We walked around and talked for a while. In the middle of the park, is a small stream. The kids wanted to go down near the water and walk across the rocks. Since they were nervous, I decided to show them how to walk across. Not thinking about going back to get Tarek, Tanya attempted to walk across the rocks in her heels. It was definitely a scratch your head moment. I did not even look. I turned my head ad all I heard was Tarek screeching (laughing). Luckily, they did not fall in.

As time went on, Tasheena and I became closer and Tanya and I argued more. I began visiting Tasheena more frequently. I can admit now that my liking for Tasheena was based off of her looks and what she had. I still felt like Tanya was pretty too, but Tanya didn't have her stuff together though. Tasheena had a house, nice car, and a good career. What could be so bad about being with her?

Life wasn't too bad. Tanya was going out doing her own thing and I had somewhere I could go to hangout and talk. So, I did. But things worsened even more with me and Tanya. I should have seen it coming. We began having heavy arguments and eventually, Tanya told me she wanted me out the house.

I was nervous. *Where would I go? To Tasheena's? My parents?* I told Tasheena about the situation and she told me to move in with her. Are you kidding? You already know what I did. I shot the deuces to Tanya and moved my ass about four miles down the road to live with Tasheena.

Looking back, it was the dumbest thing I could have done for multiple reasons. I had not known Tasheena very long, I was not completely done in a relationship, and I hadn't given myself time to heal from things with Tanya. Don't be alarmed, this isn't the last time I'll make this type of mistake. As you may be able to tell, I don't really give things much thought, and I cause a lot of my own problems.

Moving in with Tasheena was not so bad in the beginning. Tarek and Tatyanna split time between me and Tanya. However, Tarek would stay overnights with Tanya even though I had him during the day which avoided messing up his sleep pattern.

The situation worked out good for me. I never really tried to understand or ask how it was for Tanya. This is where I began to realize the damage that was done with Tatyanna socially. Because I spent so much time giving attention to Tarek, Tatyanna lacked a lot of social skills. This was not her fault. By moving in with Tasheena, Tatyanna and Alita began to spend more time together and I realized how different they were socially. Alita was outspoken. She questioned everything, not in a bad way though. Tasheena explained a lot to Alita that I would not. The way I was raised in the south was to do what parents tell you and that's all there is to it. You don't ask why or you get slapped in the mouth. But Alita was very inquisitive. She knew who she was and she has never been the type to try to be someone she is not.

Tatyanna, on the other hand, is very impressionable. She lacked a lot of social contact. Now, I understand more that Tatyanna probably seeks social acceptance more by trying to fit in, because she never had much of that interaction before.

Tasheena also enjoyed the two of them being together. She dressed them alike sometimes as though they were sisters. Tasheena was into letting kids be free. Alita dressed like a year 2030 space cadet or something. Like it was always wild and crazy day at Halloween. Alita would wear a tie-dyed shirt, pink tutu, green shorts, rainbow sox, and moon boots to the store. I would be embarrassed as hell most times. You can tell when I had the kids by myself. I dressed the children more conservatively.

It was nice though. We had fun as a new couple with the kids (minus Tarek) and we took trips out of town to Orlando, the beach, etc. When Tarek was with us, we didn't do much. We would often stay home due to my paranoia of him acting up or people staring. At his age, Tarek didn't do too well in public. He would self-stimulate a lot or whine a lot depending on crowd size or the noise level.

I was also self-conscious about how people viewed us. People, mostly men, would stare at the odd noises Tarek would make when he self-stimulated. Most women though it was cute and asked a lot of questions about him.

Tasheena was the type of person who liked to stay on the go. I think it gave her some kind of anxiety if we didn't go anywhere or if we stayed home all the time. But I've always been a homebody so it didn't bother me to be home a lot. Because it was a new relationship, I tried to overcompensate. I tricked myself into believing everything would work out. What I didn't realize, I didn't give myself enough time to get my mind healthy. I didn't give myself time to heal from the past troubles of my most recent relationship. I didn't notice a certain attitude that Tasheena had while living with her in the early stages, but I ignored the signs because I wanted our relationship to work out because she appeared to be the woman of my dreams. I was so blinded by taking care of Tarek, being there for him emotionally and physically while still giving so much of myself to Tasheena, I ignored her anxiety from not being able to go out like she wanted to when Tarek was there. To be honest, we had a blast when he wasn't around.

I don't think Tasheena actually realized how difficult it was to care for Tarek day to day. As our relationship grew, she never had the responsibility of taking care of Tarek. This created a lot of stress on me as a parent. Tarek became my shadow. Everywhere I went, he would go. If I went to work out at the local gym, Tarek took his exercise ball and sat right beside me every exercise.

When I cut the grass, Tarek would have his ball in the yard not too far from where I was cutting the grass. If I washed dishes, Tarek was in the living room or in the dining room watching me. If I went to the bathroom, I left the door open for Tarek to sit in the doorway and watch me use the bathroom.

Not doing these things caused a lot of anxiety and a lot of behavioral episodes throughout the day. Once you get those episodes started, it was very hard to turn them down.

Having to satisfy my son's emotional and behavioral needs while still trying to supply the family as a father and worker and then having to be a partner in life with someone who didn't understand the exact struggle I was going through, created a strain and extreme internal anxiety.

Tasheena grew up in Vermont. She didn't have a lot of money growing up, her mother took care of she and her brother by herself. Tasheena's friends and the people in the area that she went to school with were people that were well-to-do and had a decent amount of money.

From what Tasheena told me, she seemed to have created an expectation of life that would give her more substance than what she felt she had growing up. Because Tasheena didn't have much as a child, when she was able to do for herself, she liked to stay on the go. I failed to actually spend time getting to know everything about Tasheena before making a drastic decision to start life with her. I didn't know much about her past or her childhood. Looking back, that aspect of one's life is important to know and understand. A person's attitude as an adult is usually based on their experiences as a child. The way a person perceives and engages in relationships is likely based on their parents' relationship—whether it was abusive or a good loving connection.

When I first met Tasheena, she appeared to be nice, she beautiful, and seemed to have so much going on for herself. As our relationship grew and we gave our relationship a title, I slowly began to see her true colors. Although I didn't have any bad feelings towards her, I still caught a glimpse of a certain attitude that I didn't like. I already felt like she was out of my league, so I put myself through more emotional hoops trying to satisfy her rather than satisfy myself. It was almost like I couldn't do anything right to her ass. She could've asked me to clip her toenails with my teeth and I would have happily agreed. I cooked, cleaned, and took care of the kids. Outside of the occasional dispute, Tasheena seemed to be a pleasure to be with. I enjoyed her space and her mentality. She loved to joke around and it flowed with who I thought I was.

Around December 2012, I received an email from Tanya informing me that she was moving back to St. Louis and taking the children with her. I definitely didn't understand her message and how she can do make that kind of decision. It hurt me to the core.

As soon as I moved in with Tasheena, I started paying Tanya $250-$300 a month. I think I actually had Tatyanna more than Tanya did. However, Tanya had Tarek every night at home. Little did I know, my parents were also supporting Tanya by giving her money and paying bills for her. My mother and my father began looking at me kind of funny because they thought I abandoned my responsibilities with Tanya and left her in a bad spot. They never expected Tanya to leave either. I couldn't imagine not having my kids, no matter how much pain I was in while in the presence of Tarek. I've never felt more pain than knowing they were being taken away from me. Tanya left close to Christmas as the school semester was switching over. All I knew was I had to get my kids back.

My sexual relationship with Tasheena was kind of weird. She pretty much dictated when and how we had sex. Sometimes I was left unsatisfied, feeling less than a man because I would go too long and I wouldn't want to. There were times when she seemed to enjoy me or enjoy my presence which made me feel better, but I was never completely comfortable with the way I loved her or who I was around her. She often told me I should work out and look like guys she worked with that were buff. Often, I felt disgusting to her or disgusted by her.

Sex became more of a chore than for pleasure. Tasheena expressed a desire to have another child. Because of my relationship with Tarek and how I hadn't had a fair shot at being a good father, I wanted to try again to possibly have a son who could be more of who and how I'd always imagined my son to be. Regardless, I definitely didn't put as much thought into things as I should have.

From the time Tasheena expressed that she wanted to have a baby, we were on a sex schedule. At night after the kids were in bed, Tasheena would remind me of the importance of having sex on certain days. Being a man, I wasn't turning down sex on any day. What the hell was I thinking?!? It was clear our relationship wasn't about me at all. Why did I put myself in another screwed up situation?

As all of this was happening, I was still dealing with Tanya and trying to get my kids back. They actually lived with her until the school year ended. I never got to see or talk to them on the telephone because when I called, she would just let the phone ring. In one month, I called fifty-seven times and she answered only ten of the calls. Ten out of fifty-seven.

Eventually we went to court for a modification of the child support. During the hearing, her lawyer actually quit because of the inconsistencies in her testimony. Years late, I spoke to her attorney and the woman remembered me. She immediately referred to Tanya as "crazy as fuck." So there's that. One week after the hearing, I received a letter stating that at the beginning of the summer, I would be awarded custody of Tarek and Tatyanna due to them having more stability with me and my family.

After the kids returned, I continued going through a lot with Tarek. Like always, he battled insomnia every night. Tasheena would never understand fully how hard it was on my body to be up every night. I began to get my body in tune with his, kind of like a mother to a newborn. When a newborn baby comes home, the mother can sense the baby when the baby needs her. The baby starts moving in the crib in another room, and the mother almost has a sixth sense and is able to get up to check knowing something is wrong. This is the same sense I had with Tarek. When he'd squirm at night or murmur for my presence, I would wake up before he got out of the bed or came out of his room. There were other times when Tarek would get up in the middle of the night and stand in our doorway and call my name until either Tasheena woke me up or I went to him.

After walking him back to his room, I had to lay in front of the bedroom door to keep him from continuing to walk out of the room. If I allowed Tarek to walk out of the room, there's no telling what he would've done. He's always had an aggressive nature and would bite you, scratch you, and anything else while you sleep. Tarek would often use the bathroom in his pull-up while lying in the bed. He would then dig in the pull-up and scratch his face or wipe feces all over the bed during the night.

Many times, I woke up in the middle of the night smelling a stench. I quickly discovered I was covered in feces along with Tarek. Situation like this always made me lose control of my temper. I didn't want Tasheena to think of me as an animal. So for a long time, I didn't show the frustration I actually had.

I still viewed Tarek as "normal" and I treated him as such including in how I disciplined him. It was nothing for me to grab a belt and strike him repeatedly. Just from being awakened in the middle of the night, to waking up at 3 AM, I'd be furious. Then, elevate my frustration by waking up to feces spread all over the bed, my clothes, or on his clothes and face and I was next level insane. Tarek's legs were often red or bruised from me beating him with a belt. Each time, the more he kicked and flailed around after being hit, the angrier I got. I simply couldn't get it in my mind that Tarek was different and required a different response from me as his parent.

In a sense, Tarek was messing up my opportunity to have a normal life or at least as normal as I could get it with him included. I grew more frustrated because Tarek didn't understand the ways of his behavior. Why would you continue act out knowing what would be the result? It never occurred to me that he couldn't process it the way I expected him to. How stupid was I to overlook such a simple thing?

Even with the girls, Tarek seemed to occasionally go after them if no one was paying attention. He would scratch, bite, and pull their hair.

Just like in the bedroom in the middle of the night, I was furious because of this behavior. My disciplining Tarek became more of attacking him. There was nothing for him to do, he was much smaller than me. But yet he was so strong.

When I look back at pictures and I break down, I cry at times. I look at how small Tarek was and I think about the things I've done out of anger towards him from my misunderstanding of who he was. It wasn't fair to him. I never gave him a chance. I never gave myself a chance to figure out who he was as a child. I created false expectations because I wanted to live a certain way, and Tarek with his disability, could never reach that expectation which subconsciously frustrated me more.

We experimented with different medications to try to mellow out his moods and behavior. He developed ticks and noises that he makes while self-stimulating. I grew increasingly more frustrated.

Back to Tasheena.

She eventually got pregnant and I was expecting my youngest daughter, Mia. After Tasheena gave birth to Mia, nothing changed. The only difference in Tarek's behavior were that he never directed them towards Mia. Knock on wood, he has never laid one finger on Mia from a baby to the present day. I still don't understand the bond or significance he's created with her. When she was a baby, I'd have him hug and kiss her or even hold her. He was much gentler with her and always treated her differently from everyone else.

Tasheena, on the other hand, was the total opposite. If she heard Tarek whine, she would run and pick up Mia no matter where Mia was. She would take Mia off to another room as if she was saving her from Tarek. I didn't like it at all. I may have thought Tarek could be monstrous, but only I could think that, no one else. Besides, if she paid attention, he never tried anything with Mia and I would not have let him anyways. I began to notice Tasheena having certain looks of aggravation or frustration because of Tarek's moods. I don't know why because I was the only person really handling and dealing with him in the house. I noticed that even when Tarek was in a good mood, Tasheena would still race to Mia and pick her up if she crawled towards Tarek. Tasheena occasionally side eyed Tarek as if there was a problem.

At the time, I didn't understand what it was. In the end, Tasheena grew resentful of Tarek because he limited where we could go and things we could do because of his aggressive nature. I think Tasheena yearned for more than I could give her because of the parent I had to be to Tarek.

Of course these are my observations and opinions. It almost seemed like Tasheena grew more and more frustrated with me, creating small arguments about pointless things. Just like with Tanya, I cleaned more, I was the main cook, I could take the kids, including the baby, somewhere and she couldn't. Some of the arguments were a slap in the face for all the things I'd done. Because of Tarek's insomnia, he'd get up in the middle night and someone had to be with him. I was always that person. Tasheena could lie in the bed and sleep normally if she chose too.

While Tasheena and I were together, I could never break free from Tarek long enough to get my mind right. I probably could have noticed that Tasheena wasn't the best person for me either.

When Tasheena was pregnant with my youngest daughter, we got married. Reflecting back on it, our entire marriage was difficult. I was constantly stressed and didn't know what to expect from anyone, including my wife and my son. Sometimes, Tasheena came across as bipolar, kind of like Tarek. Just like when I was with Tanya.

14.

I pretty much know I'm a horrible person. But I couldn't stop all the anger and frustration from building up. I felt justified for everything I was doing. Nobody close to me knew or understood what I was going through.

Of course Tanya knew, and my parents knew a little bit. Sometimes I would listen to Tasheena complain about her frustration with not being able to do much or just being unhappy. She was so inconsiderate, selfish, and misunderstanding. I mean who in their right mind would tell someone who's dealing with the difficulties that I was dealing with, that you aren't unhappy or stressed out about anything. Hell, even though I knew she didn't understand, I'd still bend over backwards just trying to make things work.

After Mia was born, Tasheena barely gave me any attention. We had sex maybe once every two weeks. In fact, the last year we were together, we slept together twenty-four times, if that.

Of course she'll probably blame that on me or my lack of doing something but how could anybody live a normal life when day-to-day, the whole mood could shift because of the weather and Tarek feeling uneasy.

Even to this day, rainy days or bad weather in general are always rough days for Tarek. With satellite TV, you get the worst reception in bad weather. This has sent Tarek on tirades including banging his head on the floor so hard it just bounced up in the air. Then I'd press his head back down onto the floor repeatedly and repeatedly and repeatedly as he screamed at the top of his lungs.

I know you're wondering how I could be so mean and insensitive to the poor child's disability. If so, it's likely because you have no understanding of what my world was like back then. You didn't have to stay up twenty-four hours while still trying to maintain a normal working life. Not to mention, I live in South Georgia, there are no resources and no information. I was figuring the shit out on the fly. I mean, what the fuck was I supposed to do?

Keep in mind, this wasn't every now and then either. These were pretty much daily episodes. Episodes that I handled alone while being married to someone. Tasheena came into our relationship with hopes that she could change Tarek with the resources from her military benefits. It was a total shut down once she realized there were no resources to benefit from where we lived. What I expected more than anything was to have my wife at least know how to ease my mind when we were alone, given how much I had to deal with in terms of Tarek. But that wasn't the case. In all actuality, Tasheena complained much more than I did. In fact, I think I've barely complained openly throughout everything because most of my complaints were from not knowing what to do and just hurting mentally. I knew I couldn't continue to live life in that way. Of course, given these dynamics, our relationship soured. It soured so much that Tasheena would threaten to break up with me at times out of sheer frustration. I got to the point where I couldn't take it anymore. There was a lack of sex, lack of empathy, and a complete lack of understanding. She was completely ignorant to what I was going through.

After maybe three years together, I finally decided to leave. I explained that I thought it would be best if we separated. Things weren't going the way we expected and we weren't seeing eye to eye. What was the point of dragging things out?

The last day we were together, I remember Tasheena drinking in the living room while I was in the bathroom shaving. I was getting ready for my next day at work because we were supposed to go to the gun range and that's one of the few things I was actually looking forward to.

Tasheena came and stood in the bathroom doorway. She looked very standoffish, her feet were shoulder-width apart and her head tilted down looking up at me. Her eyes were glossy, speech was slightly slurred and she began questioning me about my decision to leave her.

I didn't really understand why she was questioning it because she'd constantly threaten divorce. Maybe because I came to that decision on my own was the problem. I should've been smart enough to "read the room" because she was visibly upset. But I wasn't too bothered, even with the conversation. I was actually kind of nonchalant about the whole issue.

I can't remember the conversation in its entirely but when it ended, around 9PM, Tasheena stormed out of the house through the kitchen door towards the garage. When she slammed the door, it shook every window. Now I've already mentioned my son's insomnia and how easy it is to wake him and who usually stays up with him when he gets up. But then remember there are also three girls in bed asleep as well.

More scared that she would wake up Tarek or the other kids, I ran to the door, swung it open and yelled, "Don't ever slam the door with these kids asleep in this house!"

Tasheena stormed back over to me, walked up the steps, and poked me in the forehead, cussing and fussing the whole time. Then, she started wildly punching me. I was more caught off guard by the punches because they didn't really hurt. But to keep both of us from getting hurt, I grabbed her and held her arms by her side without squeezing her. I held her tight enough so she couldn't escape but yet, she also wasn't able to hit me. Somehow, I don't even know how she did it, she kicked off the wall by the garage door and we both fell to the kitchen floor.

She grabbed the step stool and hit me in the face with it then jumped up and ran around the countertop. I looked up to find Tatyanna and Alita standing in the hallway crying because they heard the commotion. I jumped up and slammed close the garage door so hard it swung back open. Tasheena threw the house phone handset at me but it fell against the wall and broke.

The only thing I thought about in that moment was her

mix of alcohol and anger. I needed to go to the room to secure the guns. I'd just packed them up before the argument because of my planned trip to the gun range the next day.

Of course I didn't want her to go to the guns so I went to the master bedroom area and blocked the doorway. I never grabbed the bag, I just didn't want her to shoot me.

Next thing, I heard Tasheena on the phone telling someone I hit her and threw her down. She continued stating that I was getting my guns and was going to shoot her. I slowly walked around the counter just to see or try to hear better who she was talking to.

I heard the 911 dispatcher over the line which shocked me. I cried out to her to stop with the madness because I was gonna lose my job because of what she doing. This was one of the rare moments I didn't think about Tarek and his problems or where I've had a blow up without Tarek being somewhat involved. Tasheena continued taunting me, telling me I was going to lose my job…blah-blah-blah.

I called my supervisor hoping he would be able to help me but he was of no help. So I called my parents and let them know what was going on and of course they were on the way immediately.

When Tasheena saw the patrol car pulling up to the driveway, she taunted me again as she walked out to go greet the deputy. Not to mention, what made this much more embarrassing was that the responding police agency was the one that I actually worked for. In shock, I stood waiting for the officer to come into the house after speaking with

Tasheena on the front porch.

He peeked his head in and began speaking as if he didn't know me. Once he recognized me, he loosened up and then asked me questions about what was going on. As I explained to him what caused it and what happened after that, Tasheena who was initially outside, burst through the door continuing to curse at me while in in the officer's presence.

I explained to the officer that her behavior was what I'd been dealing with that night. I told him to notice that she was overly hyper and I hadn't done anything to cause it. The officer also then attempted to calm Tasheena down, at which point she began cursing at him, telling him that he wasn't gonna do shit because we work for the same place.

The officer then asked me to step outside. So as we stepped outside and I again began explaining to him what was going on, Tasheena burst out the door again cursing and fussing at me and the officer.

The officer told me to hold tight outside while he went inside to talk to her and calm her down. Once the officer came back outside to speak with me, he asked if I'd put my hands on her. I explained to him that I didn't. However, I told him I had to grab her because she was punching me and we both fell.

He asked if I knew where the scratches on her body came from and I told him of course not. He then detailed two small scratches, one on her wrist and another on the top of her foot, scratches that didn't break the skin nor leave a significant mark. I explained that I had no idea how she got the markings because we didn't do anything to the point where she should've got marked up, even during the scuffle.

Apparently, Tasheena told him I threw her over the counter top. I asked the officer to look at me, a 6'2 280-pound man and Tasheena, a 5'6 160-pound woman. I reminded him that we'd worked in the jail together. Using common sense, if I'd thrown, wouldn't he think I would leave more than a scratch on the wrist and a scratch on the top of her foot?

The officer told me it didn't look good because I couldn't explain the scratches on her body. Hoping he wasn't saying what it sounded like, I asked if he was telling me I would be going to jail. He told me I would if I couldn't explain the scratches. Needless to say, I took a trip to jail that night.

After I was placed in the car, Tasheena was going to be set free. So when the officer went back to speak to her, I heard a lot of ruckus inside the house. Apparently when the officer went to explain what was going on, Tasheena continued to curse and fuss at the office to the point where she continued to badger him about not doing shit because I worked for them. This was even after he told her I was in the car going to jail. Next thing I know, Tasheena is walked out of the front door in handcuffs and placed in another car.

I didn't know exactly what would happen with all of the kids still in the house but my parents had arrived so I knew they'd be okay.

When my parents went inside to get the kids, Tasheena explained to the officer that she didn't want my parents to get all of them. Tasheena told the officer that she wanted her friend to get Alita and Mia, so Tatyanna and Tarek went with my parents. This upset my father because he didn't understand why Tasheena would say or do something like that as they'd been more than welcoming to her.

This was the night I'll never forget. Because of who I was, I couldn't be held at the jail where I worked, so the sheriff's office sent me to a neighboring county until I went to court the next morning. Once I got to the jail, I was treated just like everyone else. I was booked, photographed, fingerprinted, etc. All the routine stuff. I put on a jumpsuit, which was a top and bottom, put on slippers, and they took me to the medical unit where I was held because of my status. It was probably the longest six or seven hours I'd ever spent anywhere. That next morning I was taken to court where I was released on my own recognizance.

Even after leaving Tasheena's home, she was petty. Eventually to the point of wanting gifts back that she'd bought me for Christmas.

Ever since I moved out of my parents' house with Tanya, I never expected to be living back there, especially given the situation. That shit hurt like hell, but my parents were kind of happy about it. Not because of the situation but just because the grandkids were living there.

15.

Being home with my parents had its ups and downs. My parents are good people. They went above and beyond to make sure the children and the grandchildren were always taken care of. But in some instances, especially for me, that can be burdensome. One of the grandchildren was a creature of habit. Even if those habits were extreme behaviors. The constant pacifying of Tarek caused more problems. My parents and I bumped heads a lot when it came to how they were grandparenting the children. They did not understand my view on how it was hurting Tarek in the end.

My parents got all the grandkids anything they wanted and more. Whatever Tarek wanted, he got. Juices, pancakes, chips, popcorn, etc. He even got those things when he was misbehaving. So the behavior he was displaying was reinforce by the preferred items he received. For me, this was extremely hard because I was the one in the end who had to deal with the behaviors. My parents didn't like the way I disciplined Tarek, but every time he misbehaved, I would either be used as a scare tactic or I would have to control him physically for them.

This was very frustrating because I was trying to escape some of the responsibility since I had people around me who wanted to be there for us. I guess I expected them to do more even if it wasn't their responsibility.

Tarek continued to be destructive of property and self-injurious. Even before we left the house with Tasheena, Tarek developed a tick of some sort. Tarek would make noises every thirty seconds or so. You probably think that's minor but imagine something that annoys you occurring on a regular basis. Think about having a pot in the sink and someone leaves the water dripping slightly. Imagine the first drip hitting in the bottom of the metal pan. Eventually, enough water drips and it becomes a drip and then a plop into the water. So now imagine if your child was that pot of water. Sometimes the sound would get louder and louder, depending on the situation. It will start off unintentional, just his regular tic. But then, you notice that it's getting louder and more frequent and feels intentional. Especially if I was giving someone or something else attention. If I didn't respond to his noises in anyway, it would result in misbehaving. Even at times, responding to him resulted in behaviors. Even if you respond to him positively mid-sentence, and as you speak to him, he will cut you off with those loud sounds that are annoying you to the max.

Think about the sounds that are occurring all day, in combination with behaviors, and both of you dealing with insomnia. Back then I didn't consider Tarek or his disabilities like I should have. But it was so difficult. I found myself physically restraining Tarek from destroying property or hurting himself or others for more than five hours a day. I would have to lay on top of him just to calm him. Sometimes he would even go to sleep with me on top of him. It's like he needed that deep pressure to feel comfortable. So after working a full day of work, imagine your off time being consumed by you physically restraining your child until bedtime that night. Because if you didn't, he would destroy the house. A lot of times I had to feed him myself because I would have to wrap him like a burrito in a blanket and take him to the table just so he would eat properly. If I didn't, he would slap his food on the floor or on the wall, depending on the day. It may sound cold but there is a real struggle when trying to care for someone you don't understand. And if you aren't in the best physical, emotional, and mental space, it's even worse. I was going crazy, having a massive mental breakdown.

At that time, the only way I could find peace was to drown out the sound of everything around me. I would walk around listening to music through my earbuds and then cover the earbuds with earmuffs.

It was my small bit of refuge. But it came at a cost. I'd miss conversation with my parents and if Tarek said something and I didn't respond, because I didn't hear him, he'd act out which made me crank up the volume even more.

16.

Suicidal thoughts start to settle in as my home life continued to take its toll on my mind. I couldn't keep living that way. I was still holding Tarek down for hours and had to be around him constantly. My personal life was nonexistent and I have minimal help and support. I didn't feel love for myself and if I'm being 100% transparent, I wasn't emotionally connected to Tarek by that point. I did not want to be around him and needed a release.

After leaving Tasheena, I met a woman named Alicia. I was not looking for a relationship or anything complicated, just something to help fill my sexual needs. I kept my relationship with her completely separate from my troubles at home. She knew about Tarek and the problems I was having.

Like everyone else, she wanted to help, but I continuously told her there's nothing she could do. Eventually, things between us simmered down and slowly came to a halt. Not because I didn't enjoy our time together, I just felt she didn't fully understand what was happening in my life. Over time, it she seemed to want more time with me. Time I couldn't give her. In the end, I didn't want her to feel used because I couldn't give her what she needed in return for the sex and time that I needed. I cared for her and her feelings.

Since I didn't want a relationship, I told myself that if I had any dealings with a woman, it would be strictly on a sexual level. Then I met Latoya. Well technically, we already knew each other. I first met Latoya when she worked as a nurse for my children's pediatrician. Later, Latoya started working as a nurse at the jail where I also worked. I thought she was pretty but figured she probably had a bad attitude because she was standoffish. As time progressed, we grew as friends. I never had any indication that she liked me in any way other than being friends. So when Latoya noticed me going through rough times, she reached out.

In the beginning, she may have reached out for her own sexual reasons. Because that is where our relationship pretty much started, on a sexual level. We both knew what we wanted and what we didn't want. I didn't want commitment, only freedom. I explained my situation with my son, even though she already knew from overhearing stories at work.

I broke things off with Alicia but I would occasionally still see her. I made it clear that I wanted to remain friends even though we still spent time together. Because at the same time, I was also spending time with Latoya. For me, things were excellent. I didn't have to dedicate myself to one woman while still being available at home for my son. I didn't have to worry about who should get more time.

My mother and I took Tarek to get a psychological

evaluation at the Marcus Institute. Once we completed the evaluation and I explained to the therapist that Tarek's behavior was severe, they suggested we admit Tarek to their behavior intervention program.

The program would last twelve weeks and he would have to be there every day. Initially when the idea surfaced, I was opposed because Tarek with miss school and it wasn't geographically gonna work. We lived close to the Georgia-Florida border and the program was in Atlanta. I didn't have the money to stay in a hotel and I didn't have family I could live with in Atlanta, so I declined the offer.

Months later, as the issues persisted, I decided to place Tarek in the program. Thoughts of continuing to spend days at a time holding Tarek down and not having a real social life, changed my perspective. I was prepared to live on the street just to put him through the course. Once I made the decision, I created a GoFundMe account. I explained the circumstances and I received around $1500 from Facebook friends. I used my FMLA leave, which was probably around four weeks. I've never stayed at a hotel for an extended period of time so I didn't realize how fast and how much the expenses would add up.

In Atlanta, we stayed in a modest hotel in Buckhead. After a week and a half or two weeks, the $1500 was gone. I didn't know how I was going to sustain financially, but I was going to do something. I met with Judy Aaronson, one of the resource coordinators at the Marcus Institute. She was an angel sent from Heaven. She provided me with several resources including having my insurance company pay for my time in Atlanta and another company to cover my hotel stay. Wow!

When Tarek started the program at the Marcus Institute, I was able to see that I wasn't the only person dealing with the behaviors. I witnessed so many children on different ends of the spectrum. I saw some behave wildly while others were more childlike. From what I could see, some of the parents were kind of like Tanya in a sense. Even though they were seeking help, they did not want their children to be seen in a negative light. But then some other parents looked downright distraught.

The program included Tarek attending for about three to four weeks by himself. In the first couple of weeks, they gained his friendship by giving him things he likes only to later trigger behaviors in the later weeks. This was to analyze the behavior and assess the severity. They would later include me in the program to help create distance and to implement the plan they were trying to put in place. Because I was essentially free between 9AM and 3PM during those first few weeks, I took full advantage of it.

Judy also put me in touch with respite providers. I don't know how much they were paid but these women were very enthusiastic about providing respite care. Even after seeing Tarek's behavior, they were still willing to take him. Even though one or two of the ladies may have lived in a questionable neighborhood, I didn't much care. I didn't think twice about where they lived or where they were taking him, as long as I got a break. In total, I used respite care maybe four or five days and sometimes I had to pick him up early because of his behavior.

I hate thinking back to what kind of situation I put my son in by sending him somewhere and not having any idea of where he was going. I didn't even ask questions when he returned. Again, I didn't care. I cared *for* him but as long as someone could help, I didn't care how they had to do it.

While Tarek was at respite some weekends, and even when he wasn't, I would have visitors come to help take my mind away from what I was going through.

Alicia would come one weekend and then Latoya would come the next weekend. But they had different ways of approaching our time together. Alicia was a bit flashy and wanted to go to all of the notable spots in Buckhead that she'd seen on Black Hollywood television. She wanted to go to Lenox Square Mall, Saks Fifth Avenue, etc.

On one occasion, we were eating at The Cheesecake Factory and Tarek had an episode with his respite care provider. While she was on the way to bring him back to meet me, Tarek had an episode in her car and somehow messed up her ignition. They were stranded in Decatur in the middle of traffic. So of course once I got the phone call, I was ready to go. When I told Alicia what had happened, she asked if I wanted to finish eating first. After I explained to her in a more aggressive tone that I needed to go, she then insisted on getting a refill of her strawberry lemonade. It upset me and changed my view of her.

I don't believe her insensitivity was intentional. It's just an example of how oblivious she was about my struggles. I asked for the car keys and told her I'd wait for her outside. I sat in the car for fifteen minutes until I finally saw her walking back to the car with a bag in her hand. Inside the bag, I recognized a cheesecake container. I was furious with how much time she took, especially to order cheesecake considering they were stranded on the side of the road!

After we found them and picked up Tarek, I paid to fix the woman's car, which was about $500. I paid even though she could file to get it fixed through the company but it would take longer for her to get the money. I paid because I really didn't want her to wait to get her vehicle fixed and I felt obligated since it was my son that caused the issue.

While putting Tarek in the car, I saw the bag with the cheesecake. I glanced inside expecting to see two containers, one with her preferred flavor and the other with mine. Instead, I only saw one container. After everything, she'd only bought herself a slice! I was beyond done with her.

But with Latoya, our time was dramatically different. She didn't care what we did as long as I was happy. She would even take Tarek on walks when he had tantrums, just to calm him and me. We didn't have to spend money and go to all the fancy places to enjoy each other's time. That's not to say we didn't spend money. Latoya kind of talked me into retail therapy. She knew nothing was making me happy so she encouraged me to buy something to try to feel better, and I did. I realized I felt a little bit more confident because I was doing something for myself for once.

Latoya and I would take long walks in Centennial Park and basically enjoy laid-back natural fun. Somehow, she knew exactly what I needed to get through the emotional hardship I was going through. Her value to me skyrocketed as a friend. I grew an emotional attachment to her, while still not committing completely.

I made another female friend when I was in Atlanta, too. Her son was in the behavioral program. The first time I saw her, she looked completely frustrated and stressed. But I also thought she was attractive even in her most frustrating moments. Her son, Evan, looked like a walking muscle. I don't know what his actual condition was, but I think Sheena told me he had autism. I saw her a few times walking in and out of the building, always chasing after her son. Every now and then, we locked eyes. Almost like we knew what the other was going through.

Then one day, Sheena walked up to me and spoke. When we went out to eat, we shared stories and experiences of our kids. We were extremely excited around each other. Neither of us had experienced having someone understand what we are going through outside of family. Even though I was appreciative of Latoya, Sheena was able to share something with me that most others didn't. We shared a strong mental bond. We shared a struggle with bad disciplining skills. We share the same psychological trauma from trying to be good parents. We'd both contemplated suicide. We both considered giving our kids up to the system. And we still had no idea of what to do or what our next steps would be. Whenever we spent time together, it was always in a loving and emotional way without sex. Tarek and I have even stayed overnight with her at her home. We both knew about each other's dating situations and didn't want to impede on those situations. However we shared something with each other that we knew no one else would understand.

Even though I was receiving plenty of female attention to distract me from my current issues, I still struggled mentally. One night in particular was almost my breaking point. Just like always, Tarek was in the middle of one of his meltdowns. Even with the earbuds and earmuffs on, I could hear the constant screaming in the small hotel room. Struggling to hold him down because I was so frustrated, I eventually began to swing Tarek in front of me while I sat on the sofa. Tarek was standing and going wild. I yelled at him to stop and pleaded with him, begging him for peace while still growing angrier and angrier.

In the mist of us tussling around, I tried to grab his hand, while he was scratching, biting, and swinging at me. I pushed him to create distance but when I pushed him with the force that I did, he hit the floor and hit his head. Panic set in because Tarek was on the floor, his eyes and mouth open, but he was not moving. I've never seen Tarek that still, and I knew he was not playing a joke. I yelled at him to get up knowing something was wrong. I began crying and pacing because I thought I'd killed him. I called Sheena because I knew she would understand. I explained things, stuttering and speaking fast. I'm sure I wasn't making any sense to her. I don't know if she thought it was a joke but she chuckled as if I was joking. I immediately hung up on her. I always traveled with a gun. I had a PT 111 stored in the safe under the TV. Thinking about where I work and not wanting to do life in the system for something so horrendous, I grabbed the gun from the safe and I checked the magazine to see if there were bullets still in it. I placed the magazine back in at the gun and prepared for what I had to do. I cried as I slowly opened my mouth and placed the gun inside. I tasted the bitter spice of the gunpowder around the front of the barrel from not cleaning the gun the past two times I'd shot it. I tried to pull the trigger but it wouldn't engage because the safety was on. I slowly lifted the safety making the gun active. I slapped myself in the head with the gun asking myself how could I be so stupid. I placed the gun down on the sofa. I grabbed Tarek off of the floor and cried and kissed him as if I didn't do anything wrong to him. In all honesty, I deserved one of a few things at that moment. One was to go to jail. The other was to lose my own life. The more I caressed him and kissed his face, the more cowardly I became in not wanting to kill myself. But I didn't know what to do.

While still crying over him and rubbing his face, I didn't realize that his eyes had closed at some point. Tarek began moaning. I felt multiple emotions all at once. Disgust in myself, relief because my son was alive, and scared because I didn't know what damage I'd caused. I called my mom and explained the situation. I made it sound like Tarek yanked away, fell, and hit his head. My mom isn't crazy by any means, I'm pretty sure she had some idea of what may have happened. She wouldn't get too deep into what happened, she just told me not to let him go to sleep right off the bat because he obviously knocked himself out.

That was probably the scariest day I've had ever, and it was all my fault. After that, Tarek could pretty much do as he pleased with the exception of biting and scratching me. Even if he attempted, I wouldn't get too physical with him. I would wrap him up in a blanket like I used to do and lay him down to try to soothe him in some way. Sometimes it'd take hours for him to calm down. I didn't want another night like that one even though I knew Tarek was okay and back to normal because he was doing his usual tirade on a consistent basis.

That night also impacted my thinking in other ways. I contemplated suicide more now than even especially because I didn't want to hurt him again and I didn't want to keep hurting. But for some reason, I was too cowardly to go through with it. In my head, I've battled with a lot of demons. It's like the cartoon when you see the devil on one shoulder and the angel on the other. But in my case, there was a devil on each shoulder. Who would want to live like this? I didn't deserve to live like this. And what I mean is I didn't deserve to continue living doing some of the things I was doing even though I felt like I couldn't help it. I was mentally unstable trying to care for someone with a developmental disability.

What the fuck is out there for parents who have to go through this? What does the state offer to get parents help? Georgia is by far one of the worst states when it comes to raising children or adults with special needs. Insurance, as well as Medicaid, in the state won't even pay for ABA therapy for children after five years of age. The state of

Georgia has closed almost all mental facilities, institutions—
anything that can get someone help. So what am I supposed
to do? I'm a bad person either way. People tell me now,
"You're a good father, most people can't do what you've
done." Most people would never do what I've done. Don't
call me a good father because I'm not! I'm a piece of shit and
I know it.

Around the end of October, early November 2016,
things were still the same with Tarek. In the hotel room after
he'd get out of class, I was still holding him down for hours
and hours on end. If I did not hold him down, he would
throw lamps, try to knock the TV over, and destroy property
in some way. If he wasn't destroying something, he was
asleep. Even when he was asleep, he only slept for a few
hours then woke up to torment me again until I hold him
no and he'd go back to sleep.

He'd go the Institute all day and even hearing the ladies
talk about his behavior, they always had high hopes for him.
Not one time did they ever feel they couldn't reach him even
at his most troubling points. I have to say for anybody who's
never attended or visited the Marcus Institute, it is by far
one of the best facilities for information resources and
assistance that you can go to in Georgia for children with
autism.

The employees and staff are magnificent. The have
great, optimistic attitudes even knowing what to expect
going into work each day. No matter what the child does to
them, they come in with a chipper attitude no matter what.
And a majority of the workers were college students, but

they knew what they were getting into when they took the job.

One day, I noticed a scratch stretching across a young woman's face that worked at the Institute. The scratch extended from her for head down to the other side of her cheek. I asked her who did that to her and whether she was okay. With the same chipper attitude she always had, she told me it would be okay and that it's part of the job, like it was nothing. So I asked if Tarek had done it to her since she worked with him. She shrugged her shoulders and nodded yes. She then repeated that it's part of her job and walked off. Why couldn't I be more like that?

When I was re-introduced into the program to get Tarek used to positive discipline, I noticed he was not fully cooperating with the system the workers were trying to implement. He would play the game a little bit and then once he got aggravated, he'd act out like always. He never grasped the concept of waiting or he wasn't willing to wait or cooperate.

One thing I noticed about the system in which they attempted to train him, was it didn't seem conducive to a natural home setting. The system that was going to be implemented seemed more for parents who did not work a job outside of the home. It was a lot of tracking and documents, in combination with the hand over hand work with the child. My energy, mentality, and tolerance were at an all-time low. Trying to incorporate notebooks, reading, and a bunch of other activities that involved me were not going to help my situation at home because I did not have the time, energy, or patience to work a fulltime job and come home and be super dad.

After I explained my concerns, a new plan to come back to the hotel room for treatment was created. This would really test the program because like anyone, Tarek knew the hotel or the house to be a comfort zone where he had no expectations of working for preferred items. I figured it would be problematic because of who I knew Tarek to be, and I knew where the problems would lie based on habits that were enabled by loved ones. Hell to be honest, I wanted them to continue at the facility and not invading my space. I wanted them to set up one of the rooms in the facility as an actual home setting but I guess that's my fault for overthinking things. Man oh man, when I tell you, when Tarek was re-introduced into a homestyle comfortable setting like the hotel, the gates of hell came down and Damien was reborn. I think they tried this for about two or three weeks. Each day of those weeks, Tarek proceeded to rain hell down upon them.

I have a few of the incidents videoed on my tablet. Tarek bit, kicked, and punched those ladies everyday they came. They women would enter like the Dallas Cowboys or something—with helmets and arm pads everywhere.

After seeing his behavior consistently, the therapist wanted to extend the program, but I couldn't do it. I couldn't continue to take the drive and Tarek was not making any progress. Not from a lack of effort. Those people wanted their work to make a difference and they desperately tried. But I couldn't continue to drive three and a half hours for what I could endure at home. Earlier in the program, while heading to Atlanta, it took me seven hours to travel what normally would take three hours because Tarek had a meltdown on the side of the road and I had to call the crisis hotline numerous times. He tried to kick my dashboard in and then he tried to kick the window out.

I had to jack him up out of the front seat, which he had to ride in because you didn't want him behind you, into the floorboard behind me and fold him up just to calm him down. Stuck on the side of the road, crying and frustrated with the crisis team on the phone, the police stopped because they noticed us stranded, commotion happening inside the vehicle, and Tarek folded up in the back.

I explained to the police what was going on and I also explained that Crisis Team was supposed to be enroute. The officer explained that he thought it would be too dangerous for us to remain on the road so he would follow us to the nearest exit. Once we got off the exit, the police went in the opposite direction of us and was quickly out of sight. How frustrating. The police saw us and my child in the floorboard and he still took off. I couldn't continue to go through that anymore, so I decided to withdraw Tarek from the course.

17.

After returning home, nothing was improving personally. My parents continued to be in denial about the severity of Tarek's behavior, ignoring what was resulting from their enabling. Initially, they failed to see exactly how it was affecting me. Of course they knew about the incident at the hotel, but they still saw and ignored my mental downward spiral. As my frustration grew, I think my parents worried more and more. They knew I had to be the disciplinarian, and if it went too far, they would always be there to step in, if needed.

Truth be told, I always needed them to step in, but I would never say it. I felt it was my responsibility to make sure Tarek did what he was supposed to or what I expected of him. No matter how many times Tarek couldn't do what I asked, I still expected it.

Months after attending the Marcus Institute, I found myself doing the same things that I was doing before and during those rough times. I was still holding Tarek down for long hours of the day. I was still mishandling him due to frustration. I can't remember exactly how many times I called the crisis line of Georgia, but they became so familiar, they knew exactly where to go and all the details. I didn't know what else to do and I didn't know if they were going to take him away from me or if they were going to send people to help but I needed something and I needed somebody to help me.

Calling the crisis hotline was kind of tricky for me at first because I didn't want it to seem like I couldn't handle my own child. However, I wanted them to know the severity of the behavior. I tried to hide my mental frustration as well. But after multiple calls back to back multiple times a week, I finally broke down. I explained to the crisis team that I was at my wits' end. I explained to the crisis team that if things were to continue, and with my fragile mental state, I was afraid I'd hurt Tarek. When they asked me to explain what I meant by hurt him, I explained to them that when I try to restrain or discipline him and his temperament goes up, so does mine. And when it gets to that point, I was afraid I would unintentionally hurt him to the point where he can't come back. I was scared I might kill him.

The seriousness of my claim and my concerns forced the crisis team to intervene. Tarek was taken and placed into a crisis home for adolescents about forty miles away in Tifton, Georgia. Initially, I didn't know how to feel about it. Personally, I needed the space and the time to get better for myself and for him. But I felt like a failure. How could I let my son go into the system?

The crisis home offered things a normal household setting couldn't offer. Tarek had constant supervision from people who took shifts and swapped out while working with him. This is beneficial because it gives people time to de-escalate and gather themselves at home. They had time to relax and come in and be able to give Tarek the proper care he needed. What hurt me was I never had that break, I never had anyone that could relieve me when I needed it.

Tarek stayed at the crisis home for about a year, give or take. While he was there, I moved out of my parents' home. I didn't know if I would ever return to my parents' home and I didn't know if Tarek would come back home either. I didn't know what the next step was but I wasn't trying to think of what the next step was going to be because I wanted and needed space from him. I needed and deserved it. I knew Tarek was okay because the state had him in custody, but I worried about him constantly.

My parents and I could visit him anytime we wanted. It was only thirty minutes away so my parents visited quite frequently. In the beginning, I struggled to visit. Toya and I were getting serious so she would take me to visit Tarek. In the beginning when I began visiting, sometimes I never even went inside. They never knew I was outside in the driveway. This crisis home was situated in a regular neighborhood. It was a house that had been altered inside to keep children from being able to hurt themselves or hurt others. Breakaway doors, windows without blinds, etc.

When Toya took me to visit, she would pull into the driveway and my hand would start shaking. She would see me sitting there pretty much having a panic attack. She took me multiple times before I actually ever went inside the house.

When I finally worked up enough nerve to go inside, I wouldn't stay too long. Now I had the option to remove myself when I felt overwhelmed. Whether it was the noise or the constant repetitive phrases that Tarek would make, it was the simplest things that would drive my anxiety through the roof. I've never felt so broken in my life. I couldn't even sit in the same room my son for more than half an hour without running for the exit. How could I be this way? He still calls for me like I've never done any damage to him.

I moved into my own place and started to work as a courtesy officer at an apartment complex. I was lucky to have a break from Tarek and the financial instability that I was suffering from by paying $1000 a month to Tasheena in child support. I didn't have a way to live independently if it wasn't for being a courtesy officer. A courtesy officer is a certified police officer providing security for an agency who lives within a complex for discounted rent. Tasheena took me to court and I was forced to pay her approximately half of my net income a month. I made approximately $1000 every two weeks. So, one of the checks I received during the month went completely to Tasheena. My parents were furious about because Alita, which is my daughter and I still love her like my daughter, is not biologically mine and even though I took the responsibility to adopt her to make her part of the family and to give her my last name, Tasheena sought a monetary opportunity to hurt me. She couldn't get anything from Alita's biological father but decided to make me financially pay for what he did not do. She was always unapologetic about it and insensitive about the lack of funds that I have to care for Tarek and Tatyanna who she claimed to still love. Tasheena went on to live in nice places and huge houses and I could barely get by. Four- and five-bedroom houses for her and both girls. Then trying to make me feel guilty for her bill amounts in these places but when I mention my financial strain, it like, "Oh well, something will come around for you."

When Tarek was in the crisis home, things got better for me in many ways. I began to elevate myself in my career. I was having a healthy relationship with Latoya. And now I could give some attention to someone who I hadn't paid much attention to over the years almost as if they were a ghost. I spent much more time with Tatyanna independently without Tarek being there constantly demanding my attention.

It's weird, I never resented Tarek, but I knew I was limited on things I could do in my life because of him. I didn't know if I liked traveling because I had rarely been able to go anywhere. I didn't know if I liked going out to places because I was always with him. With the break from him, I learned that I love traveling and I love going out. Without the thoughts of suicide and the limitations that I'd had, it gave me a new understanding and value for the opportunities in my life.

Toya opened me to many new facets of life. We began traveling and living outside of the norms of what most people do. I was loving it. It's almost like I had a deeper appreciation for money and opportunity and life in general. I think my experiences with Tarek and then having a break, changed my entire view of everything surrounding life in general. It even made me look at religion and spirituality differently.

I was able to hit the gym consistently. I'd let my body go throughout the years because of the inability to go on a consistent basis and work out. Now I had the time to focus on certain things that could help me stay mentally grounded, comfortable, and confident in myself. But then the question would come into my mind, why am I enjoying life so much without a piece of me? My son, that I'm supposed to love and care for, be there for, provide security for, was not in my custody and I was comfortable with it for some reason. I was actually enjoying myself knowing that one of my children was not with me. How could I do this to him and how could I be so shallow?

Although I questioned my parenting skills, or lack thereof, I continued to adjust to my anxiety while visiting with Tarek. I would force myself to be around him doing things like cutting his hair and trying to play little games with him here and there.

They explained that Tarek would have difficulties with behavior with them as well. I thought if Tarek had constant supervision, people who were able to go home and build their energy levels back up to play with him all day, he would be content. But I learned that's not all of what the situation was about. I guess it was comforting to know I wasn't the only person who had to deal with his extreme behavior. It gave me more confidence when people would reassure me that I shouldn't feel bad for enjoying my time away from him. Some of the workers and others would explain that it's important that I have time to myself, because if I didn't, there's no telling where we would be.

18.

Tarek would never come back home to live with me. When he was in the crisis home, my parents often stressed the importance of Tarek being home around family. They constantly asked me about my plan. I'd tell them I didn't have one. Over time, my parents convinced me to allow Tarek to live with them if we could find resources that would allow workers to come to their home and assist with daily routines. After multiple conversations, I eventually agreed.

So eventually, Tarek left the crisis house and moved in with my parents. Because of my love for my parents, I allowed this to happen based on their wishes. But I did not agree with them. They were getting older and were more fragile and unable to keep up, while Tarek was getting older, stronger, and more energetic. The violent nature of Tarek's meltdowns had me extremely worried. I was nervous that if we couldn't find the proper staff to assist when he had meltdowns, my parents would get hurt.

When he first got there, we dealt with multiple small agencies that provided personal care. I would often find myself still calling the crisis line to assess Tarek's behaviors.

Even with the service providers in the home now, we learned from that finding service providers for juveniles is often quite hard. We experienced that firsthand. We dealt with a lot of very small local service providers that barely could staff the home. I always wondered it many of those small agencies were committing some type of medical fraud for the way they billed for the staff yet weren't supplying staff some days.

I recently discovered a video when my parents were using one of the smaller local service providers. This is one of the most hurtful views I've seen. It was my mother and father struggling to control Tarek and restrain him in my mom's office area. Seeing my sickly, fragile mom wrestling with Tarek while my dad's arthritis-ridden body slouched over to attempt to gain control of Tarek, immediately brought tears to my eyes. To know that I allowed this to happen, hurts me to think about.

While my ass was taking trips and seeing sites, my parents were dealing with shit that I was supposed to be handling myself. They wouldn't tell me but they shouldn't have to tell me what was happening. My parents needed me and I wasn't there. True enough, they'd asked for that responsibility but in the end, it wasn't their responsibility to take and it wasn't for me to give.

While Tarek was in my parents' home, I signed a power of attorney so my mom could control different aspects of his life. My mom told me at one point that for she and my father, dealing with Tarek gave them something to do while they were retired. I guess that was her way of trying to comfort me while we continued to struggle finding adequate help.

I think we went through a few agencies before ending up with CaRes. They are a contracted service provider that supplies staff to homes. My brother, Ashley, actually worked part time with one of the agencies before eventually getting hired with CaRes. He works for the Department of Juvenile Justice and to earn extra money, he worked part-time for a behavior health company. Once he saw the need my parents had at home with Tarek, he got permission from the state to work for the service providers. This was viewed as help because Ashley could provide a sense of firmness with the way he dealt with Tarek and then Tarek's response to Ashley would be different from other workers because he knows Ashley as family.

I think my parents have had CaRes providing services for approximately two years to the present. My son grew attached to some of the workers. Some were young guys who were energetic and didn't mind taking Tarek places and constantly doing things with him. They appear to work well with Tarek even in his intense moments. Or so we thought. Even though we've had our ups and downs with CaRes, we ended up with a decent crew that my parents trusted.

They could take Tarek on outings and spend time with them and give my parents the break they needed. However, there were a lot of things my parents weren't telling me. My parents knew that if I felt that they we're being used or there were things that shouldn't have been done by staff to Tarek or them, that I would want to find an alternative to CaRes.

We had quite a few staff members. Brianna, Michael, Bruce, Trevor, Johnny Oliver, and Darnell were the in-house staff. Donna was the house supervisor. LaTessa was Donna's supervisor and Harriett was LaTessa's supervisor.

The whole goal for someone receiving services through a service provider is to provide a service that assists the family in the day-to-day operations within the home. The service provider is supposed to teach the client different life skills that assist and help make the client's life better. No parent wants to worry about their children being mistreated by anyone. I mean, I may have done a lot of shit wrong before, but I'll be damned if I would allow anybody to do anything hurtful to Tarek. The problems I had were due to trying to do things by myself, ignorance, stress, etc. But no one would envision seeking help and allowing people into your home only to have them mishandle your loved one.

So with CaRes being in the home, I thought everything was all good. I spent a lot of time working and thriving in my career knowing my mother and father had help. Later, I found out that at times, the workers weren't being accountable and coming in properly. I also discovered that the company wasn't sending other employees to cover the home. The complicated part is when my mother signed up for the services, a contract was signed saying that CaRes would be accountable for keeping staff in the home at all times. When staff wasn't available to work in the home, they should have pulled people from other places or call people who are off-duty to see if they can come in. Leaving the house unstaffed is considered negligent by law. There are no ifs, ands, or buts about it. Two people over sixty years old trying to take care of a young strong autistic kid, who was getting stronger every day. I never understood how this never became a concern for CaRes.

However, it got worse.

My parents treated all of the staff like extended family. We have had multiple family functions and the staff was always invited. They would eat with our family and never paid for anything and were never asked to pay for anything. Sometimes, I think staff forgot they were staff and at a few events, they ate before family did. But none of us minded because they were doing us a service as a family, although it did strike up conversations. Later I found out my parents had also sent money to some of the staff. They'd asked for money for various reasons that I have no clue about. I have checked my mother's Cash App and found the transactions that she sent to numerous staff members. Some of the money was incentives for just being there for work, being there on time, being good staff, etc. But I think my parents spoke too soon and didn't know the true intentions or actions of certain staff members.

In the beginning of 2020, COVID-19 began making a stir across the United States and the world. With my parents and my son being high risk, my mom held a meeting with all of the staff members to discuss proper protocol when dealing with the virus. She hung signs on each door and put sanitation stations throughout the house. She told them the cleaning requirements and even had thermometers to take temperatures. She informed staff that all persons who lived in the home were high risk and if anyone came in contact with someone with COVID-19 or anyone that exhibited symptoms of the virus, to not come in the house. Again, my mother specifically held a meeting and informed all staff and CaRes management that no one who came in contact with someone with COVID-19 or exhibited symptoms themselves or tested positive regardless if they were asymptomatic, was prohibited from entering the home.

Time went by and not many people took precautions as seriously once we got to the summer. We had a couple of our good staff quit for no apparent reason. One of the staff members in particular was Trevor. He was one of Tarek's favorite people that worked for CaRes. We treated him like family. So why the hell would Trevor quit out of nowhere? What could cause him to leave?

Now just to give you an overview of Tarek's services, CaRes was contracted to provide two-to-one care during the day and one-on-one support at nighttime. His behavior was so extreme and he was so hyper that during the day, no one person would be able to do the job efficiently. In our area, Tarek is the only minor actively being serviced by CaRes. He also receives the highest amount of funding currently with CaRes. At one point, Tarek's annual funding was around $250,000. His daily routine usually consisted of going out in the community to parks and learning life skills and independence.

I don't believe my parents ever had a clear understanding of where Tarek was going most days. According to CaRes, employees are supposed to fill out logs detailing all the trips and times of when they go anywhere. At times, Tarek would be gone an entire shift between six to eight hours. It all depends on the day and Tarek's behavior.

Based on conversations I've had numerous times with workers, even when going out on day trips, Tarek was still exhibiting problem behavior. This poses a problem because Behavior Analyst recommended that when Tarek exhibits behaviors, he needs to come straight home. He doesn't need to be out and about because he can injure himself or other people. Also, it becomes a problem with staff if Tarek has his problem behaviors inside a vehicle and he gets physical, it could be a danger to the driver and the person in the back that's trying to help de-escalate.

On March 24, 2020, LaTessa sent my mother a document. It was for staff to refer to when entering my parents' home based on new COVID-19 standards.

On April 2, 2020, LaTessa sent my mother forms the staff had signed based on the new COVID-19 standards. The signed papers were meant to acknowledge that all staff understood the rules that had been created.

On April 7, 2020, my mom held a phone meeting with all CaRes staff and management. The call was in reference to COVID-19 pandemic protocols. In that meeting, my mother advised and discussed with everyone participating her concerns. She explained how she can be greatly affected if the staff does not take proper precautions when considering her pre-existing conditions. During that same meeting, my mom explained that she did not want any staff in the home who'd displayed symptoms or tested positive for COVID-19. My mother also stated that even if a staff member was asymptomatic and tested positive, she still did not want them in the house because they still risked passing COVID-19 to the next person and they may not be asymptomatic when they catch it. All staff and CaRes were aware of my mother's wishes and concerns.

Like I said, my mother created multiple documents and cleaning procedures for everyone to follow when entering the house. She also bought cleaning and sanitation materials for the staff. She was trying to ensure that nobody could come into the home and infect her, my father, or Tarek.

On June 10, 2020 CaRes created an update for COVID-19 protocol. CaRes advised that staff members could continue to work inside the home if they are asymptomatic.

Now this is where things conflicted. Just a couple months back, my mother held a meeting explaining her concerns and her high-risk based on pre-existing conditions and then CaRes told their staff that they could enter my parents' home. Not a CaRes's facility but my mother and father's home against their wishes.

My parents had made it clear but for some reason, CaRes decided they could supersede my family's wishes in their own home. So I'm pretty sure you can tell where I'm going with this.

Earlier I mentioned that my brother worked for CaRes. He was actually in the staff meeting with CaRes. He heard the Human Resources Supervisor and LaTessa tell staff that they did not care if you tested positive or not, you were to return to work as normal, as long as you didn't exhibit any symptoms. This was even confirmed to me by one of the other staff members.

Roughly a month later, on July 16, 2020, Tarek began showing signs and symptoms of COVID-19. Staff was advised to document the symptoms and conditions, in which they did. He continued to display signs and was tested at Smith Northridge Hospital on July 17, 2020.

Tarek received his results back on July 18, 2020, which resulted in a positive test result for COVID-19. Unbeknownst to the family, some of the workers, Michael, Oliver, and Brianna, were routinely taking Tarek to their private homes or places that had not been authorized for Tarek to visit.

There are many complications and liabilities that come from Tarek having contact with unauthorized people. People who have not been properly trained to handle him and his disabilities could result in Tarek or the person being hurt or killed.

Donna, the supervisor over the staff, told me about an incident where my mother was called by Michael and Oliver due to the van having a flat tire. This incident occurred about thirty miles away from the family home. In Adel, Georgia to be exact. Adel was not an authorized location for Tarek to be so why was he there? After my mother arrived on the scene, she noticed Tarek and the staff outside of the vehicle with numerous unknown people from the community.

My mother explained that Tarek appeared comfortable around unknown persons as if he's been in contact with them people before. She said the area smelled like marijuana and she noted that they weren't in the best of neighborhoods. This was in fact a high drug and crime area. No one was ever written up about this, nor was staff provisions created.

So why would a special needs child with autism be anywhere near any of that? What could possibly be an excuse for them to take him there? It's obvious they were visiting people because they weren't authorized to be there anyways. Do I know that for fact? I don't but it doesn't take a rocket scientist to figure that out.

My only concern was that if Tarek was around somebody and bites or scratches them, what might that person do back to him as a result? It's clear the staff wasn't taking the same precautions with Tarek's life. I guess with my mom speaking so highly of them, I expected the staff to treat Tarek more respectfully. LaTessa and Harriett were made aware of the situation and nothing was done. No new rules were made, no consideration for Tarek, no new precautions or rules were made around the vehicle, or how they should transport him from there on out. This situation demonstrates the lack of care that the staff was exhibiting with Tarek in their custody. Their actions were going to hurt our family dramatically.

Later it came out how Tarek contracted COVID-19. One of the male staff members, Michael, took Tarek to his grandfather's home in Valdosta. Now Valdosta is a common place for Tarek to be because that's the next biggest town closest to Lakeland. No one ever gave anyone permission to take Tarek to their homes especially because of the new

COVID-19 precautions. I discovered that at the time that he took Tarek to his grandfather's house and his grandfather had COVID-19.

Michael had also made statements to other staff members that he was quarantined from his son because he was around his grandfather and he exhibited some signs of COVID-19. Michael was still attending work regularly.

After Tarek tested positive, the staff called an emergency meeting. On the same day, Michael and Brianna did not show up for their 3 PM to 9 PM shifts. During the staff meeting, Michael voiced his concerns about why staff had to continue to work with Tarek and he was in quarantine. Michael, Oliver, and Brianna would refuse to work for the next few weeks or so. But Michael was the same person who was staying away from his own son for safety purposes yet took my son around people who were exposed to COVID-19, including himself.

With Tarek's positive results, the staff was directed to quarantine him to his room and keep him away from my parents. They stated that they did not feel comfortable since Tarek was positive for COVID-19. These are the three people who have been taking Tarek to unauthorize places around unauthorized people. I don't know if it was guilt or what, but you take my son to all these places and then once you expose him and get him infected, you fucking run away?!? How disrespectful and cowardly is that? Not one time has either person admitted any of it except when in the presence of other staff members that they trusted.

One of the other staff members overheard Michael

talking to his mother on the phone about all the people in the family that were presently diagnosed with COVID-19 and that he knew he himself had it. I don't understand how you so easily put someone's family at risk when they explained just how high-risk they were. What bothers me more about this is how much CaRes management knew but chose not to address or fix it. They knew Michael was positive and allowed him to work in the home after my mother stated not to. We trusted these people to take care of my family's needs. I thought they would at least respect the home and the people who lived in it. But I guess when you're making all that money for my son's funding, who gives a shit...

The first couple days in August, Michael, Brianna, and Oliver returned to work. Right after the staff had an emergency meeting, everyone was tested and Michael tested positive. When Michael returned, he never obtained a negative result before coming back into the house.

So Michael and another staff member were going to take Tarek on an outing that day. When my father asked Michael where he was going, he explained that first, he was going to the hospital to be tested for COVID-19 and then they were going to the park.

My father called LaTessa and explained that he didn't want Michael back in the home if he hadn't had his testing done. By this point, my mother, who was extremely high-risk, started exhibiting symptoms of COVID-19. The staff knew she was on at-home dialysis. My mother had complications with her heart and her kidneys. They all knew about her conditions for the past couple of years that CaRes was the at-home service provider. This was not any new news to anyone.

My mother will eventually have to go to the hospital where she will be admitted. She will never come home from that hospital stay.

> Elder abuse is an intentional act or failure to act that causes or creates a risk of harm to an older adult. An older adult is someone age sixty or above. The abuse often occurs at the hands of a caregiver or a person the elder trusts.
>
> Neglect is the failure to meet an older adult's basic_needs. These needs include food, water, shelter, clothing, hygiene, and essential medical care.

My mother of course had preexisting conditions that made her admittance into the hospital more important. My mother was admitted to South Georgia Medical Center at the end of July. At the time, she was fully competent and aware of her surroundings. I spoke to her frequently via cell phone towards the beginning of her stay.

During the early stage of being at the hospital, several issues arose. One of the first problems was that my mother constantly spoke of were inconsistency of the nurses providing her with her dialysis treatments and not knowing the steps to process her dialysis treatments. I spoke to my mother almost daily during that time. At one point, she asked me to bring her home dialysis machine because the nurses were not providing her with the treatments in a timely manner and maintaining a sterile field. She expressed concerns of getting peritonitis. She even called her dialysis clinic to inquire if they could come carry out her dialysis during her hospital stay but was told by her dialysis clinic that they are not contracted by the hospital and would not be able to do so. The clinic also informed her that patients often incurred infections during their hospital stay.

WHAT HAPPENS IF DIALYSIS IS DELAYED?

Without dialysis, toxins build up in the blood, causing a condition called uremia. The patient will receive whatever medicines are necessary to manage symptoms of uremia and other medical conditions. Depending on how quickly the toxins build up, death usually follows anywhere from a few days to several weeks. Some of the most common end-of-life kidney failure signs include: water retention/swelling of legs and feet, loss of appetite, nausea, and vomiting, confusion, shortness of breath, insomnia and sleep issues; itchiness, cramps, and muscle twitches, passing very little or no urine, drowsiness and fatigue.

My mother also commented on the quality of the food. So, Latoya and I began preparing meals and buying food from the local restaurants for her to eat. We were not allowed to see my mother or go up to her floor of the hospital. So when I brought food to her, I would park in the parking deck, enter the parking deck entrance, and give the food to the greeter. The greeter would mark the food and place it on the table to be picked up whenever staff was available.

No one knows how long the food sat on the table. I later learned while talking to my mother, that in the beginning, she was getting her food on time. But eventually, she would receive the meals later and later from the time I dropped them off. I tried to drop them off around the same time every day. My mother also stated that sometimes her food would be at the nurse's station and she would have to ask for it.

Latoya and I were married shortly after my mother was hospitalized. She was a floor nurse at the time of my mother's admission and stopped by her room and noticed that the fruit and sandwich that was purchased from the grocery store the night before was in a chair across the room and my mother was unaware that it was ever dropped off. I became concerned, especially when the staff began explaining that my mother began not having much of an appetite and was not really eating. For days, nurses would report that she had not eaten anything all day.

As time continued, my mother began having trouble with her oxygen and breathing levels and was restricted to a BiPap (bi-level positive airway pressure) breathing apparatus which required assistance with feedings. A BiPAP machine is used to maintain a consistent breathing pattern at night or during symptom flare-ups in people with COPD.

I asked if I could be allowed a visit to assist with feedings while she was on a BiPAP mask because of staff shortage and was constantly denied visitation by my mom's physician and nursing staff. At this time, nurses were stretched thin and techs were assigned one or two to a floor and sometimes no one was available to help with feedings. My wife can attest to this having worked there during that time.

For about a month and a half, my mother did not eat more than a pound of food in total. I repeatedly asked to visit to assist with her feedings and was constantly denied. Nursing staff and my mom's doctor attributed some of the appetite issues with stomach pains and confusion (delirium).

Delirium, also known as acute confusional state, is an organically caused decline from a previous baseline mental functioning that develops over a short period of time, typically hours to days. Delirium is a syndrome encompassing disturbances in attention, consciousness, and cognition. It may also involve other neurological deficits, such as psychomotor disturbances (e.g. hyperactive, hypoactive, or mixed), impaired sleep-wake cycle, emotional disturbances, and perceptual disturbances (e.g. hallucinations and delusions), although these features are not required for diagnosis.

Dr. Anderson and the nursing staff informed me of my mother's delirious state. I asked many questions in reference to this for weeks because I was extremely concerned. The hospital advised me that my mother could not tell where she was or identify her family. When I spoke to my mother at times, she did not appear to be in the same mental state as I was being told. During our conversations, my mother would talk about the nurses not talking to her and being rude as if she wasn't competent. She explained to me that she felt alone.

I asked numerous times if the delirium may have come

from being in constant solitude. Nurses and my mom's doctor would agree that her mental state could come from no social contact. I asked how they expected her to get better if she never has any social contact with anyone. I would never receive a response about it. I began explaining the concept of Psychoneuroimmunology (PNI) to the staff and the doctor. Psychoneuroimmunology (PNI), also referred to as psychoendoneuroimmunology (PENI) or psychoneuroendocrinoimmunology (PNEI), is the study of the interaction between psychological processes and the nervous and immune systems of the human body.

During a brief conversation with my mother, she told me that she knew what she wanted to say but just can't say it. I took it as she was aware of what was going on but was unable to put the words together to make a statement. I noticed that my mother also seemed forgetful during conversations. She asked me once, "Is she here today?" and was unable to put a name with who she was referring to. I would say names in an attempt to help her recall whom she was speaking of but it didn't always work.

What I do not understand is how a patient can get well with no nutritional intake for physical growth and healing. No social contact for mental stimulation for close to two whole months. She was not in a psychiatric ward or a prison. What grounds gives a hospital the right to hold a patient hostage like they have been with little to no familial contact? Family has no way to contact or see their family who is admitted to aide in the care of their loved one. Staff advised me that the rules were based on CDC guidelines, I looked up CDC guidelines and the rules the hospital implemented:

According to the CDC, visitors are strongly discouraged from visiting patients who are at increased risk for severe illness from COVID-19. If visitors are allowed, facilities should follow national policies regarding the use of medical masks or face covers (e.g., homemade mask) by healthy visitors. Visitors to areas where patients with COVID-19 are isolated should be limited to essential visitors such as those helping to provide patient care and/or caring for pediatric patients. Limit to one visitor/caregiver2 per patient with COVID-19 at a time. Caregivers are defined as "parents, spouses, other family members or friends without formal healthcare training" per WHO interim guidance for home care for patients with suspected novel coronavirus (COVID-19) infection presenting with mild symptoms, and management of their contacts.

Based on these recommendations, it talks about visitors for Covid-19 patients helping with patient care. It said that visitors could be limited to one person. In this hospital's case, with the staff shortage, why would you deny visitors for a patient in need of care? In my mom's case, a familiar face could have assisted her with eating, going to the bathroom, and social interaction. She was bedridden after suffering a cerebral stroke limiting movement on the right side of her body, A BiPaP mask limited her mobility as well and prevented her from eating her food regularly. My mother's hospital stay was torturous.

But in the end, I feel the greatest weight of guilt. None of this would've happened if I would've done my job as a parent. If I would have had Tarek in my home instead, there wouldn't have been anybody to take him anywhere to get my mom sick. CaRes is definitely at fault for what they've done and the hospital is at fault for what they've done but I'm also at fault. I feel like a horrible son, a horrible person, and a horrible father to all of my kids. No one has to bear the pain that I have borne from my lack of responsibility. I feel like in the end, I killed my mother. This could've easily been nonexistent if I would've stepped up and done what I was supposed to do. So while I'm out trying to have a career and trying to spend time with my other family, I left my parents hanging and one of them suffered with their life.

What makes this much worse, is after my mother died, Trevor called to check on Tarek. Remember he was my son's favorite staff worker that quit out of nowhere. During the conversation, he asked who was bathing Tarek. Donna asked him why. This is when Trevor explained that he quit because Michael, Oliver, and Brianna were beating on Tarek, smoking weed around him, and were constantly meeting people to smoke with while with Tarek. They would go the parks and sit behind the softball fields out of sight from the public. Trevor explained that it all started with Michael, then Oliver, and they convinced Brianna to start hitting him.

From there, the meltdowns at the house started to make

a lot of sense. Most of the time, Tarek would only attack those three. Management knew many of the issues because I would call them about it with proof. I even put a GPS tracker on their company van and monitored them taking Tarek to their homes multiple times for well over three or four hours. No new rules were put in place after reporting everything to management. Staff barricaded Tarek in the van with a blue floor mat to the point where he couldn't move. I sent CaRes management the pictures of it. Nothing was done, no new rules were put in place.

I had to quit the job I'd held for almost ten years, because after my mother's passing, I was told it was my job to pick up the slack when CaRes didn't find staff. But they were being contracted and paid to do just that. CaRes hasn't been filling the employment vacancies after I exposed all of the staff-related problems we've experience. I was told I would have to find the staff for the home because they couldn't find anyone who wanted to work at my parents' house. Yet, I posted the job on Indeed and received over twenty calls in two days from potential candidates. CaRes told me they posted the vacancies but couldn't find anyone in almost three months. For that entire time, they worked with four staff members. For perspective, typical staffing is twelve people. I gave CaRes twelve applicants to choose from and only two have been hired. CaRes has and continues to put my family through so much shit its ridiculous.

They took away some of my son's services because of the things their staff did. They promised my mom a van for transportation and took it away later claiming he was not supposed to have it. And the van was approved by the supervisor and was there for a year. When will my family catch a fucking break?

19.

My relationship with my son has always been complicated. Nobody fully understands the complexities behind our relationship. I wish someone could see it the way I do, but then again, that would just give me more of a reason to justify things that I've done in the past.

Everything I've done for Tarek, I thought was for his greater good. I wanted Tarek to be as "normal" as possible in the end. When I leave this earth, I don't want Tarek to have to rely on people to help him. I was trying to protect him from the very people that I turned out to be. My intentions were good but my actions were not.

Tarek has affected many relationships that I have with different people. I find myself a lot of times trying to justify why I am the person I am in my social awkwardness. Even with my other children. To my three girls, I apologize. I always tried to be better than what I turned out to be. I hope I gave you a clear example of who not to look for in a partner in life. I hope you find somebody who is more patient and more mentally capable of dealing with troubles that you may face in your life.

I feel most sorry wasted a lot of valuable time that I could've been spending with Tatyanna. I owe her a lot more than what I could ever dream. For all these years, she played a ghost in the background. Anytime she tried to get some attention, Tarek would spoil the moment and act out. The behavior was completely intentional because you could see Tarek watching you or try to pull you away.

I spent the majority of the days when I wasn't with her mother, entertaining Tarek or managing his outbursts. As a result, Tatyanna developed her own troubles in some ways. She had to figure out how to navigate social crowds without parental help. She had to go to school with limited help from me as a parent. I mean, imagine coming home from a day of school and wanting to spend time with your father but he's lying on top of your brother for five hours until his bedtime. When Tarek lived with my parents, it gave me a chance to be a better parent to Tatyanna. But as a result of the trauma that I had been dealing with, it didn't do any good. A lot of times, I would hide in my room with the door closed because I desired silence. I desired to only be with myself, in my thoughts. Most times, I didn't even want to hear myself thinking. So even though Tatyanna and I were the only ones in the room or in the home, she still was by herself. I still don't know how to actually have a relationship with my daughter.

Even now, it's like we have an awkward relationship. Like I don't know who she is even though I do. And I think it's the same from her perspective as well. I think she's trying to figure out what type of relationship she can have with me and we're both looking at each other trying to figure this thing out.

With Mia and Alita, it's a little different. Alita didn't know her father growing up and yearned for a father figure when I first met her. When her mother and I finally got together and I got used to the person Alita was and her personality, I almost felt like I knew her better than I knew Tatyanna. But I don't even understand how that's possible since I've had Tatyanna in my life longer than I had Alita.

Alita and Tatyanna are two different people. Alita was comfortable doing her own thing and making her own style. She was very vocal and expressive. Tatyanna is the complete opposite and I wanted her to be like Alita a lot of times. I had to learn that Tatyanna will develop into her own person sooner or later. The reason she did not know how to make friends or talk is because of the lack of direction and parental guidance I provided.

I see Alita no different than Tatyanna or Tarek. We might not share the same blood but she is my child. I've grown to love Alita more than I ever thought I would. What hurts most is that now I can't really have a relationship like I want to with them.

After Mia was born, I wanted so much to rewrite all of my wrongs. I tried to shower Mia with affection. Mia seemed to prefer my presence over her mother's. It's not that she didn't want her mother's touch, I think it was about the goofiness that I brought to her that she enjoyed.

Sometimes I found Tasheena jealous of the relationship she thought Mia and I were creating. I can't say it was malicious but maybe it was innocent jealousy. When Mia was a baby, she could just climb on my stomach and fall asleep with her head on my chest easily. Whereas, Tasheena had to fight with her to go to sleep.

Once Tasheena and I separated, she appeared hellbent on separating the family in a sense. From the night we both got arrested, Tasheena allowed all of the children to be separated by having Alita and Mia go to a friend's house.

After we went to court to try to settle the legal dispute, Tasheena wanted to get back together, but I didn't. I felt that if she called the police that quickly on me for something I did not do, the next time it will stick. I wasn't going let that happen to me again.

She worked in the military and was an active reservist. It would be almost impossible to get orders to be sent somewhere against your will. Tasheena knew I always wanted to live near the ocean on a beach or close to it. She moved to Pensacola, Florida. Even after moving there, she continued to try to get me to move down to be with her. It was tempting, but I still decided not to.

This made seeing the girls that much more difficult. I can only see them once every two weeks, if possible. Still only surviving on half of my income per month. She would run guilt trips on me to make me feel as if I'm not doing enough when I truly couldn't. I had Tarek, the lack of attention and attentiveness that I wasn't giving Tatyanna, not having the money to travel four hours to go see Mia and Alita, and she never once tried to see it from my eyes. And honestly, she never had to move in the first place, she decided to go. Why would she take the kids away from me knowing how difficult it would be for me to ever see them or spend time with them? I'm sure that wasn't her thought or concern.

I barely have time to think about the complications myself and as soon as I try to figure out a plan to see the children more, I get more surprises. Tasheena decided to move to the Washington, DC area, even farther away. How the hell would I see the kids regularly? This made a bad father an even worse father.

I realized that my relationship with my children wasn't a concern of hers at all. Deep down I still wish she would have some sort of sympathy at least because of Tatyanna. Truth be told, I don't think she ever truly liked Tarek. To this day, she still doesn't really ask about him but she will for Tatyanna.

I remember the first time I saw Mia after they moved to the DC area, she might've been two or so. When she moved away she was just a baby. I expected her not to know who I was and thought she would've forgotten about me. After knocking on the door to their house, I noticed her walking around the corner. She paused and stared at me. I reached my arms out to her and she allowed me to pick her up. She didn't forget about me like I thought she did. Sitting down with her on the sofa made me cry more than ever, because of the time that I was losing watching her grow.

Presently, Tasheena and I actually have a decent relationship. We are both in relationships and I still don't think she understands my troubles. I am semi-forced to watch my daughters grow up from a distance. I don't have access to the same money that she does. She has her income, half of my income, and her fiancé's income. While my household only runs off of my wife's income and half of mine.

But whenever the children go to the doctor or to the dentist, I'm sent the bill to pay half in addition to support and I have to arrange to try and get the kids when I can. Regardless of my financial situation, I try to get the girls as much as I can, as often as possible. But it's hard because even when I have them, I still pay the support to Tasheena. It is what it is I guess. I mean, there isn't shit I can do about it. I can't see them like I want to because of having to be accessible for Tarek. So what's a person to do? How can I be a good father in a situation like this? If anybody has a good answer, please let me know.

*   *   *

My relationship with my family has gotten better over time. I try to approach things from a calmer mind frame. Even with Tarek's outbursts, I don't react like I used to. But I'm nervous that I'm not ready to be all-in again but I need to be for my father. My relationship with my father probably took the biggest hit through the years.

He always thought he knew best and he thought I overreacted. I think he starting to see things differently. He's beginning to see how frustrating certain things can be. Now that my mother is no longer here, he understands the process more than ever. He can't grieve properly because of Tarek's presence in the house. Because of Tarek's demands of attention. These are the same things that messed me up all these years.

I never got a chance to grieve for my grandmother, my uncle, and I technically don't even know how to grieve now given my mother's death. When my grandmother died in hospice, my mother wanted me to bring all the children up to see her. When we got there, my mother tried to share the experience with Tarek in seeing my grandmother. He had an outburst and slapped my mother across the face and proceeded to have a tantrum because he couldn't do the things he wanted to do at that time.

My dad is not as judgmental now because he swapped places with me, and he's the one having the breakdown. Now we spend time talking and sharing responsibility of what happened to my mother, his wife. Truth be told, my mom couldn't have come back into the house anyway. Not with Tarek and his lack of understanding. Not after her having two strokes.

Tarek is terrorizing when he doesn't get his way. It's almost like he is bullying the workers and my dad. My dad gives him what he wants because he doesn't want to deal with the behaviors. My father feels like he needs Tarek there for his own mental health. I don't know how long he can continue to do this with Tarek, but he continuously stresses to me that he doesn't know what to do without him and he doesn't want me to take him away. I hear him but he can't handle Tarek, they never could. I don't know who can handle the ongoing aggressiveness.

I reflect on my absolute disappointment with CaRes. We sought help and CaRes signed a contract saying that they would take on the responsibility to assist and support our family. However, CaRes put my family in more troubling situations than they should have. They still don't care or accept their responsibility. But against my parents' wishes and better judgment about having infected people coming into their home, CaRes allowed their workers to enter my parents' home knowingly being diagnosed with a deadly virus. It resulted in my mother getting sick and eventually dying a horrible death.

Instead of addressing all of my concerns and strengthening their protocols and systems, CaRes wants to act as though nothing happened and rid themselves of me as a client. My son was being abused by staff physically. My mother died because of the ignorance of the staff. Yet they refuse to service my son properly because of the problems their staff created.

Then there is the school. How can a state facility continue to disregard the needs of special needs kids? My son has been in the school system for eleven years and he still isn't getting the proper help that he needs. I tried to get them to send him to better schools before, but now because they don't want to deal with his outbursts and aggression, they are willing to send him off somewhere. Because they are tired of dealing with the behavior that they also enabled.

All of this time that has been wasted when we could've found better resources and other places, but I was denied. Now that he's bigger and stronger and more violent, now they finally see the problem. I've sent letters to the White House trying to reach Michelle Obama. Crazy thing is, I got a letter back from one of the staff members telling me to refer my complaint to the state of Georgia.

I've sent letters to Holly Robinson Pete and Rodney Peete, Ellen, Dr. Phil, etc. You name them, I have sent a letter. I've tried to get help for almost a decade. To see the news and all the bullshit that goes on day-to-day, it's heartbreaking to know the true issues are being ignored.

I don't know what to do from here. You look at the news and all of the political drama. But you never see anybody discussing real issues going on in real people's lives. Mental health is one of the biggest issues in America right now. The biggest mental institution in Georgia is the prison system. Let that sink in. The government cuts all mental health funding but keeps their gas cards. Then people who aren't even able to care for themselves properly are placed in the system because people don't want to deal with their issues. That's a real dilemma. But they're limiting all resources and funding. Georgia is one of the worst places to be with a child with autism. So what are the parents left to do, especially with children who have extreme behavioral issues? I can't describe the feeling of being a parent with a child with autism with no resources, but then you can turn on the TV and watch celebrities brag about the progress that their autistic children are making because of the things that are available to them.

I'm not blaming the celebrities because I understand that they've made a lot of money over their career from hard work. It's just stressful and hurtful to see that it's possible that your child could have things that will make them better but you will never get access to it. So again, what are the parents to do?

Personally, I've been at the end of my rope. The past few years I made progress mentally but I still have some issues. Death doesn't scare me like it used to. In fact, I sometimes find myself jealous of the peace I think people have when they pass on and leave me here. It's not that I want to die or anything, I just yearn for a sense of psychological and mental peace. I want to know that my son in actually being taken care of with no worries.

The people you get into relationships with, they want the best for you. The problem is, for me, they never understand the struggles I encountered before ever meeting them. They are usually full of energy and enthusiasm when I'm usually the opposite. It's hard pleasing someone, when there's nothing pleasing about your life. I don't know what is in store in the near future, but I can't say I'm looking forward to anything. I take life day to day.

I'm hoping that this book can shed light on an ongoing problem in society. There are so many parents making the best out of bad situations. I am not one of those people. I'm hoping *Missing Pieces* provides conversation to people in high places who can make resources available so that new and current parents who may face the same problem I did, won't make the same mistakes I did. I hope the future holds something better, because I still have a lot of pieces missing inside of me, and I don't know what to do.